Born to Fly

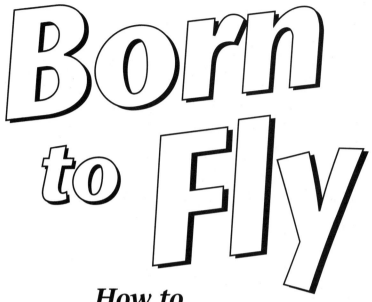

Born to Fly

How to Discover and Encourage Your Child's Natural Gifts

Thom Black

with Lynda Stephenson
Illustrations by Mary Chambers

ZondervanPublishingHouse
Grand Rapids, Michigan

A Division of HarperCollins*Publishers*

Requests for information should be addressed to:
Zondervan Publishing House
5300 Patterson Avenue S.E.
Grand Rapids, MI 49530

Library of Congress Cataloging-in-Publication Data

Black, Thom
 Born to fly : how to discover and encourage your child's natural
gifts / Thom Black, with Lynda Stephenson.
  p. cm.
 ISBN 0-310-40281-6
  1. Parenting. 2. Child rearing. I. Stephenson, Lynda
Rutledge. II. Title.
HQ755.8.B58   1994
649'.1—dc20   93-47962
                                                     CIP

Published in association with Sealy M. Yates, Literary Agent, Orange, California

Designed and edited by Blue Water Ink

Cover design by Jody Langley
Cover illustration by Mary Chambers

Printed in the United States of America

 94 95 96 97 98 99 00 / ML / 10 9 8 7 6 5 4 3 2 1

To

Debbie and our children,

Joshua, Talia, and Megan

Contents

Preface

SOMETIMES I think we have life all backwards. Maybe when we get done saving the world we all will return to activities like playing in the sandbox and building forts out of sticks. Maybe the natural energy of our children tells us more about where we are going and what we have been designed to do than have all the things we've learned during our years of formal education and informal experiences.

I wrote *Born to Fly* as much for me as for you. It scares me to think that messy bedrooms, unfinished homework, or some other source of frustration may cause me to lose the fascination of watching my children emerge as real people. I remember the wonder and amazement I felt when Debbie and I brought each one of our three children home from the hospital. Those are feelings I don't want to lose. So I've written a book for both of us about our kids.

I've always had a hard time sifting through page after page of tightly packaged text to extract one or two obscure ideas from books crammed with inaccessible information. That's why this book is "user friendly." We've highlighted the important ideas so they are easy to find as well as easy to understand, and we've used lots of artwork to help make the book entertaining as well as educational.

I would like to thank the following people who have made a difference in this book: Richard Johnson, Paul Lewis, Sealy Yates, James MacDonald, Karen Sawyer, Janet Roos, Lisa Kuntz, Charlotte Ferris, LeAnne Pauley, and Mary Ashipa. I also acknowledge Sun Tzou, a military strategist who lived three thousand years ago; his insights into warfare were inspirational in chapter six.

Special thanks to Lynda Stephenson, who patiently coached me forward and invested a bit of herself into the project; to Mary Chambers, a fountain of creativity, who captured the spirit of *Born to Fly* in her drawings; to Julie Link, who steadily guided all of our art and text and sometimes crazy ideas of how a book could look into something that makes sense on the printed page; and to Sandy Vander Zicht, who has made a career out of helping big kids fly.

Thank you all.

Introduction

Which Comes First:
the Chicken
or the Egg?

A New Way of Seeing

My business
is not to remake
myself,
but make the
absolute best of
what God
made.

—ROBERT BROWNING

arents are responsible for who and what their child becomes.

❏ **True**

❏ **False**

If you're like most parents, you believe the above statement is true. So you keep looking for the formula that will make little Johnny clean up his room, be less sloppy at the table, finish his homework before dinner, and take out the garbage on the first request. You keep hoping to find the magic words that will make little Janie pay better attention, practice her piano, be nice to her little brother, and use better manners around adults.

You keep hoping that the next thing your child does won't frustrate, puzzle, or surprise you. But that's exactly what keeps happening.

Are the following scenes familiar?

JULIE is six. She has spent three hours cleaning up her room, just as her mom instructed. Yet when her mom checks on her progress, she sees that Julie has picked up nothing at all.

"Julie, what have you been doing all this time?" her mom asks.

Julie grins, grabs her mom by the hand, and proudly pulls her over to look inside her top dresser drawer. Every item of clothing—every sock, every shirt, every piece of

13

underwear—is arranged by color and size. "Do you like it?" Julie beams.

"You've spent all this time on this one drawer?" her mom asks, sighing. "What about the rest of this mess?"

HANK is eight. He's been in and out of his room while his mother has been busy on the phone. She hasn't noticed that he has gathered together a pitcher, a handful of plastic bags and twist ties, a felt tip pen, and a cooler from the basement. Nor did she see him huddling over his goldfish bowl catching goldfish with the pitcher, pouring them into separate bags, twisting the bags closed, and then writing the name of each goldfish on the side of the bag.

14　　By the time his mother wonders where he is, Hank has

already set up shop in the front yard and is doing a brisk business selling his fish for ten cents each to the neighborhood kids.

MICHELLE is nine. She likes to play the piano, and she plays very well for her age. Her teacher awards her the spotlight in every recital. She has one problem though. She plays everything fast, *very* fast. Whenever her teacher and her mother scold her about this, she ignores them. One day while she is practicing, her mother, for the hundredth time, tells her to stop because she is playing ridiculously fast.

"Why do you insist on playing so fast," her mother asks in exasperation.

15

"That's what I like the most," she smiles.

"What do you mean?" her mother says. "Don't you like the music? This piece is supposed to be played s-l-o-w-l-y, Michelle."

"That's boring." She starts playing the piece as fast as she can. "I like to see if I can play it faster than I did last time," she yells over the din, grinning from ear to ear.

Parents spend a small fortune buying books to find out what they can do to make their children act . . . right. Experts have made a science out of raising children; they've devised strategies and theorems, whole bodies of psychological concepts on the subject. And most of what they say has the ring of truth. For example:

16

"TRUTH" #1

Children are blank slates on which parents doodle, creating what and who their children become.

"TRUTH" #2

The order in which children are born into families determines their personalities.

"TRUTH" #3

Every mistake parents make wounds children deeply, often resulting in emotional scarring that requires hours of psychotherapy later in life.

Talk about truth or consequences.

Yet despite all the expert advice, moms and dads are still trying to get kids to do the simplest things. Rooms are still messy, chores are still undone, brothers and sisters are still fighting, homework is sloppy, and kids continue to behave as if they have lost their sense of hearing. They obviously haven't been listening to the "experts."

The universal parental question

The moment children are wheeled out of the delivery room, parents become obsessed with one question:

What should we do?

- ✳ If we let him cry through the night, will he turn into an axe murderer?
- ✳ If we feed her on demand, will she turn into a self-indulgent yuppie?

Questions like these never get answered; they just become more complex as children grow.

WHAT SHOULD WE DO?

It's like that old riddle: Which comes first: the chicken or the egg? What is most important in raising a child: what the kid is like or what the parent does?

The experts all around us would have us believe the secret is in what we do . . .

☞ **THE TEACHER:** "I'm sorry, but your son just doesn't seem to be interested in what we are doing in class. You should do something about his having:
   a. too little energy
   b. too much energy
   c. a nose for trouble
   d. a learning disability

☞ **THE DOCTOR:** "As you can see from the chart, your daughter is . . .
   a. too large; you should put her on a diet.
   b. too skinny; you should feed her like a horse.
   c. too tall; you should squish her.
   d. too short; you should stretch her.

☞ **THE PASTOR:** "Your child is strong-willed and needs to be taught to love God. Failure to do this will . . .
   a. doom your child to a godless life.
   b. doom you to a lifetime of guilt for failing to raise a god-fearing child.

Responses like these, though perhaps well-intended, are detrimental because they perpetuate the mistaken idea that there is such a thing as a perfect child. And so parents, who seem to come equipped with a mental list of what a "good kid" is, continue their never-ending quest to find something that doesn't exist: a magic formula that will make their kids turn out "good."

19

GOOD KID · GOOD KID

LISTENS TO
  PARENTS
WELL-MANNERED
GOOD STUDENT
EATS VEGETABLES
DOESN'T FIGHT
  WITH SIBLINGS
HAS CHARMING
  HOBBIES
NEAT

DOESN'T TALK
  BACK
DOES CHORES
  CHEERFULLY
TIP-TOES DURING
  MOM'S NAP
SHARES TOYS
SELF-MOTIVATED
PREFERS CLASSICAL
  MUSIC

Yet no matter how good our intentions are, how high our expectations are, or how long our lists are, our children still flutter.

> **flut-ter,** *vb., to move rapidly and irregularly; to be in agitation or uncertainty; to throw into confusion.*

This is a fact. At one time or another children all act crazy, illogical, strange, silly. They frustrate, scare, and anger us. And once again, we ask, "What can we do to make them perfect?" Why can't we have kids who don't drive us up a wall, who do what we say, who live up to our good kid quotient?

Science or art?

Contrary to popular opinion, raising children is not a science. It's an art. Also contrary to popular opinion, parenting is more about the children and who they are than about what parents do to make them toe the "good kid" line.

Lists won't work. Ultimatums won't work. And even goals won't work because they are YOUR goals.

Formulas won't work because they belong to strangers who have never even met your child. There isn't a formula written or a list created that can determine what each child will be.

Why?

Because each child is like no other. Your child is absolutely unique. He or she was born with unique abilities and with unique ways of responding to experiences. Just like you were. And nothing you do, nothing others tell you to do, can change that—because the Creator made our children; we didn't. And what the Master Designer makes we can't change with lists, good intentions, high expectations, or psychological theories.

21

What difference does this make in understanding our children?

Before we can get past the puzzlement and frustration, we must recognize that each of our children is a one-of-a-kind package of abilities. When we acknowledge our child's individuality, we also will begin to understand why he or she sometimes flutters.

Why do kids flutter?

Although many parents say their main concern is what kind of person their child becomes, they often are more interested in whether the child does what they expect him or her to do, giving almost no thought to what the child naturally does.

When kids have to do things
that don't come naturally,
they falter and flutter.

———————

Yet the same kids, when
allowed and encouraged to use
their natural strengths and
abilities, soar.

Look at the following list of things your child may be expected to do today.

- ❖ **Finish homework alone**
- ❖ **Give a speech in front of classmates**
- ❖ **Listen to being called names**
- ❖ **Deal with striking out at bat**
- ❖ **Share a favorite possession**
- ❖ **Straighten a messy room**
- ❖ **Write a thank-you letter**
- ❖ **Play nicely with EVERYONE**
- ❖ **Go through an entire day without making any mistakes.**

How in the world can we expect any kid to do all these things well? Let's be honest. How many of us did all these things well at their age? How many of us do them well NOW?

Some of these activities your child will do well naturally, just as we do. These abilities are part of them—like *wings*. And wings that can soar through a spelling test may flutter when the task is cleaning a messy room.

Fluttering, then, isn't willful disobedience; it's the natural response of children who are expected to spread their wings beyond their natural wingspan.

Parental expectations are natural. They just need to make sense. So here's the simple but revolutionary idea . . .

Before we can help our children soar, we need to know the shape and size of their wings.

24

We need to see each of our children as a package of strengths as well as weaknesses. When allowed to operate in their areas of strength, they will soar. When forced to operate in their areas of weakness, they will flutter.

A new way of seeing

Think back to the stories about Julie with the messy room, Hank with the goldfish, and Michelle with the fast fingers.

What was your first impression of these children:

25

Julie is . . .
- ☐ a dawdler
- ☐ lazy

Hank is . . .
- ☐ unappreciative of what he has
- ☐ looking for mischief

Michelle is . . .
- ☐ silly
- ☐ wasting her talent

These stories are typical of the kind of daily frustrations that drive parents to sigh, roll their eyes, and beseech the heavens. Julie is a dawdler, Hank is always getting into something, and Michelle is not being serious about the piano.

But there are other things we could learn about these three if we would just LOOK at them differently. For example . . .

Julie's mom could have learned that Julie is good at focusing on one task to the exclusion of everything else and has a way of putting her own stamp on what she does. Of course, she still has a problem with being messy.

Hank's mom may have learned that Hank has a natural sales ability or business sense. Or that he has a way with people. She may also have realized that Hank doesn't feel much emotional attachment to his pet goldfish.

And Michelle's mom could have seen that Michelle likes competing with herself more than anything—even more than playing the piano or making beautiful music.

This new way of seeing provides a fresh perspective on a child's actions and it can help parents respond more appropriately. We are meant to be more than critics or admirers of our children's behavior. Much more.

How are you feeling? Is frustration getting in the way of parenting satisfaction? It happens so easily. As your child grows and the issues of parenting become more complex, your initial enthusiasm is replaced by frustration, inadequacy, anger, and helplessness.

Even though I don't know you personally, I know one thing about you. I know that you are in love with your child. If you weren't, you wouldn't be reading this book.

And this book is different from all the others in your stack because *you* make it different. You make it a book about *your* child.

My goal in the following pages is to help you hold onto your enthusiasm for parenting through a lifetime relationship with your child. Throughout the book you will find tips for . . .

❖ understanding your own natural style of parenting.

❖ recognizing the abilities that make your child wonderfully unique.

❖ managing a full nest without going cuckoo.

❖ creating an atmosphere where your child's wings can unfold to their full soaring potential.

Let's Play!

This book is meant to be like a playground. Use it to teach and nurture your children as you help them discover, develop, and spread their wings. As you do, joy and enthusiasm will come flooding back into the task of parenting.

Lisa's Story

I was going to be supermom.

From the very first day of my daughter's life, I was going to do the right things—always. I set up a chart to remember the doctor's guidelines on the best way to feed my newborn. She was supposed to eat every three hours. And that's the way it would be. But Lisa didn't want to eat every three hours. We had to wake her up to feed her and then try to keep her awake during the feedings. Then, not thirty minutes later, she would wake up and want to be fed again. At first I tried to ignore her. She was going to be fed on schedule. By the book. But the crying didn't stop, and she was almost frantic to eat. After three days I threw out the chart and fed my baby by her schedule, not by the schedule of some doctor who didn't even know her. By watching Lisa I was able to sense when she needed to be fed, even what was the best pattern of sleep for her. We were learning that she knew what she wanted and needed, even at two weeks old, and what we needed to do was pay attention.

Getting STARTED

#1   Put your child's name on a notebook (or purchase a separate *Born to Fly Work- book*). You are going to record things you want to remember about your child.

#2   Tiptoe into your child's room tonight after he or she has fallen asleep and remind yourself of how precious your child is. Remember, the only time your feelings change is when your child does something you don't want him or her to do.

#3   Get ready for the ride of your life! We're going to launch you into a lifelong adventure.

Chapter One

What Shape Are Your Child's Wings?

Helping Your Child Fly

Tell me what
you like and
I'll tell you
what you are.

—JOHN RUSKIN

E ALL HAVE THEM.
Preconceived ideas, that is.
Preconceived ideas as to who our
children are and what they should
be like. Another word for this is
"expectations." Be honest. What do you expect from each of
your children? In the illustration below look for the word or
phrase that best describes your expectations for your child.

Which box is your child in?

Now let's look at those expectations in the context of the
seven commandments for helping your child fly.

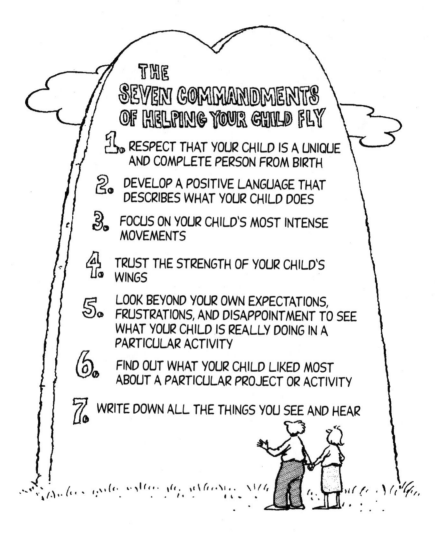

THE
SEVEN COMMANDMENTS
OF HELPING YOUR CHILD FLY

1. RESPECT THAT YOUR CHILD IS A UNIQUE AND COMPLETE PERSON FROM BIRTH

2. DEVELOP A POSITIVE LANGUAGE THAT DESCRIBES WHAT YOUR CHILD DOES

3. FOCUS ON YOUR CHILD'S MOST INTENSE MOVEMENTS

4. TRUST THE STRENGTH OF YOUR CHILD'S WINGS

5. LOOK BEYOND YOUR OWN EXPECTATIONS, FRUSTRATIONS, AND DISAPPOINTMENT TO SEE WHAT YOUR CHILD IS REALLY DOING IN A PARTICULAR ACTIVITY

6. FIND OUT WHAT YOUR CHILD LIKED MOST ABOUT A PARTICULAR PROJECT OR ACTIVITY

7. WRITE DOWN ALL THE THINGS YOU SEE AND HEAR

1

Respect that your child is a complete and unique person from birth.

ALL children have a uniquely shaped spirit. They are not made with cookie cutters, and they do not all thrive under the same conditions.

To create an environment in which they can test their wings and learn to fly, parents need to believe that each child is a unique individual with unique abilities and a unique personality.

Chisel this idea into your mind so it won't wear away:

My child came into this world with a set of wings ready to grow and spread and fly.

If we help our children develop their natural abilities, we'll enable them to fly high and far and long. If we try to make their wings look just like our own, our children may flutter their whole lives. By beating their wings they may become airborn for a moment, but they'll be on their heads the next.

Any sports commentator worth his Saturday afternoon microphone will remind viewers to keep their eyes on the ball. Why? Because if they don't, they'll miss the important action. What happens to the ball determines who wins the game.

The same advice is good for parents. When there is a flurry of activity going on *around* your child, focus your attention on precisely what your child is *doing*.

❖ If he is two years old, he is struggling to unfold his wings.

❖ If she is three and a half, she is straining to get off the ground.

❖ If he is nine, he is lifting off for short periods and crash landing at the most inopportune times.

And in all this effort, tremendous energy is being expended. You can see it on any playground. Children of all ages, in motion, doing what they do naturally, bumping into all kinds of expectations and standards set for them by adults and their peers.

As you watch all this, remember to concentrate *not* on all the activity *around* your child—not on unmet expectations, messy rooms, or poor report cards—but on the child's energy, the efforts he or she is making to fly.

He may make you loopy with his bizarre behavior.

She may try your saintly patience with her moods.

They both may make mistakes that keep you in a constant state of worry.

But it's all part of learning to fly.

Your agenda, then, is clear. As a parent, your job is to get

your child off the ground and into the air.

Are you more interested in having your child do what you think a "good kid" does rather than what he or she is good at doing?

2

Develop a positive language that describes what your child does.

WHENEVER someone asks you about your child, you do two things. First, you start rummaging in your purse or wallet for a photograph. After showing the picture, you feel frustrated because it doesn't seem to convey all of his personality or all of her charm.

Then you begin to talk about your child. Think about what you say. Do you talk about her blond hair or his brown eyes or how skinny, fat, short, or overgrown she is? No, not at all. Physical characteristics are obvious from the photo. You tell stories about what he or she *does*. You use words to create a better picture of your child than the photo you have in your hand.

And do you know what? It works. When it comes down to it, children aren't much different from one another physically. But by telling stories about what Joanie does and how she does it, you describe your child so well that the listener could pick her out of a kid-filled room. How would that person recognize her? Not by the photograph, but by words

37

describing her energy, motion, and personality, which are much more distinctive than her brown hair or blue eyes.

Our words can describe all this energy, and they can paint a bright, cheerful picture or a dark, depressing one. When we're talking to a long-lost friend or relative we tend to use positive descriptions of our children. But when we're talking to our children themselves, we tend to use negative ones.

Do these phrases sound familiar?

- ✗ *You never . . .*
- ✗ *Why won't you stop . . .*
- ✗ *Quit being so stupid . . .*
- ✗ *How come I always have to . . .*
- ✗ *Why do you always . . .*
- ✗ *How many times must I . . .*

At one time or another such phrases can be used to accurately describe any of us. But they never make us better people. And they never help us learn to fly.

Parents who want to help their children fly develop a positive language that replaces the negative one, which seems to come so naturally to us.

Where do these new words come from and what will they be?

They come from stories and descriptions you will write about your child's activities. Stories like this one:

ONE lazy Saturday afternoon when Josh was ten, he grumbled about not having anything to do. Having heard this before, we just ignored him, so he disappeared into his room. A few minutes later he came out wearing a policeman's outfit—hat, badge, sunglasses, shirt covered with police patches—and with pad and pencil in hand.

"I've got work to do," he announced as he moved through the kitchen, out the back door, and off into the neighborhood on his bike.

Two hours later, the back door opened dramatically and in strolled Josh, smug and smiling, tapping his notebook with his pen. Tearing the top three sheets off the pad, he let them float to the kitchen table. "Not a bad day's work," he said in his best Barney Fife imitation. "Fourteen expired license plates. Had to sneak through a few yards, look through some garage windows and climb over a few sticker bushes, but I got them. Think I should turn 'em over to the police? People got to remember there's right and there's wrong. And this is wrong."

Is Josh telling his parents that he wants to be a policeman when he grows up?

Not necessarily.

Is he telling them that he's going to be a righteous peeping Tom?

Let's hope not.

Was he just trying to be annoying?

It might seem so, but think about what he was doing. He was using his energy to see that right things are done and that wrong things are corrected.

One story doesn't provide enough words for a new language, so let's look at another story Josh's dad wrote. Josh was six when this incident happened. Can you detect any pattern?

On a very average summer afternoon, Josh asked if we owned a camera.

"Yes," I answered, "but what do you want it for?"

He grabbed my hand and pulled me out to the front porch. From there we could see a large steamroller rolling new tar into the street several houses down.

"See that steamroller?" Josh pointed. "When it stopped in front of our house, those men ate some potato chips."

"So?" I asked.

Josh hopped off the porch and pulled me toward the street's edge until we were standing over the new tar. Josh pointed to some bumps in the new blacktop. "They didn't pick up the potato chips, Dad. They just rolled them into the road."

"Well, why do you want the camera, Josh? To take a picture of the chips in the road?" I asked, smiling.

He nodded his head furiously. "We've got to take a picture of those men and get them fired. That was wrong to do that."

After a few stories, a pattern begins to develop that should tell Josh's parents something about Josh's thinking, what some of his strengths might be, and also how those strengths can be used either positively or negatively. It will give them words as well as actions to help Josh make good use of his strong feelings about right and wrong.

After looking at enough stories, you begin to assemble a whole language about your child's strengths. A language that does more than describe what your child *doesn't* do; a language that describes what your child *does* do. And that will lead you to know what *you* can do.

Josh's parents have been writing stories like the two above and they are beginning to see their son as they never would have otherwise.

So let's begin yours.

Exercise #1

Write three or four stories about occasions when your child was busy doing something he or she put a lot of energy into. Maybe it was building a fort, helping to make cookies, directing a play in the basement, dressing up, taking something apart, or having tea with an imaginary friend. Remember, your stories will be unique because your child is different from anyone else in the world. The key word here is *energy*. Write about some activity or situation that your child expressed some passion for.

3
▼
Focus on your child's most intense movements.

YOU'VE probably noticed by now that your child's abilities do not have equal intensity. You may also have discovered that your child has many different abilities. Out of all of them four or five will emerge as the strongest. These are your child's wings. Developed properly, they will keep your child in the air and on course. All the remaining abilities are feathers. They are *essential* for flight, but not *sufficient* for it.

A lot of career tests adults take are ineffective because they fail to differentiate between wings—our strongest abilities—and feathers—the abilities that support our work. Consequently, the results are often more confusing than enlightening.

As you watch your child and record old stories as well as new ones, you will notice certain abilities that surface over and over again. These are your child's emerging wings—his or her primary abilities—and they are the strengths you want to develop and nurture.

To do this you must control your own natural responses to see what your child is doing. I have three children of my own, so I know how difficult it is to do what I am suggesting. But by putting your frustrations on hold long enough to get a clear picture of what is going on, you will be able to respond wisely and more effectively to your child's behavior.

You must watch closely.

If all you ever understand about your child is his or her primary abilities (wings) even if you never identify the secondary abilities (the feathers that aid in flight) you still will be able to help your child fly better and straighter.

That's how important these strongest abilities are. You must learn to identify them on sight and to recognize them in all your child does before the knowledge will be of any benefit.

When you know *what* those wings are, you can learn *when, where,* and *under what conditions* they work the best.

If you worry when your child's wings don't work well in every situation, remember . . .

Einstein couldn't run a four-minute mile.

4

Trust the strength of your child's wings.

ONCE you begin to look for your child's wings, it will be difficult *not* to see them. Children are always ready to try out their wings, and not always at the right time and place. (More about that later.) What's important to know for now is that these wings—which are the most consistent and most visible expression of what your child does—tell you almost everything you need to know to properly guide your children.

In identifying your child's wings expect a simple and obvious pattern to emerge, just as we saw in the case of Josh and his natural desire to see things done the right way. These patterns will recur over the entire life of your child.

Think then how important it is to identify them as early as possible so they can be strengthened and trained to be used for good.

Words that describe your child's strengths will be:

Consistent

Repetitive

Strong

Willful

Over and over again, you will see specific things happening in the activities your child chooses. And this repetition will make it easy to develop a language that describes your child and which you can use to communicate with your child.

The next exercise is designed to help you identify your child's "wings" and to develop your special language.

What kind of wings does your child have?

In every action, there will be a consistent, repetitive energy fueled by your child's strength and will. Everything he or she does will be focused on a goal or goals, such as the ones below.*

List three things your child enjoyed doing this week.

1. _____

2. _____

3. _____

Which of the following was he or she most focused on:

My child was most focused on . . .	My child has wings like . . .
☐ **Affecting someone**	**THE COUNSELOR.** George needs opportunities to be close to others, forging relationships which go deeper than the surface. He needs to change the outlook of those he is close to, equipping them to rise above a negative situation. ***Flight Pattern:*** a need to counsel, help, assist others; a desire to be close to others; a drive to make lives better.

* For the sake of clarity, I've used boys to illustrate some tasks and girls to illustrate others, but all of them can be done by either, of course.

My child was most focused on . . .	My child has wings like . . .
☐ **Being chosen for something**	**THE CHOSEN.** MaryAnn is motivated to follow the invitation of a leader. She is devoted, committed, and loyal. Being asked to participate in a project or outing excites her and builds her self- worth. *Flight Pattern:* excitement about an invitation; the ability to fill a chosen position; a respect for position and esteem.
☐ **Interacting with other people**	**THE FRIEND.** Donny is most comfortable with a select group of individuals. He desires the diversity of having friends with different strengths, weaknesses, and interests but is most comfortable enjoying them one at a time. *Flight Pattern:* a desire for one-on-one interaction; a delight in meaningful conversation; a need to meet new people.
☐ **Meeting a need someone had**	**THE HELPER.** Stephanie knows what others need. She can enter a situation and determine what is necessary to achieve a goal. She reaches reach out to those who are lacking and tries to transform their living conditions. *Flight Pattern:* the motivation to identify and satisfy specific needs; the drive to better others' lives; the desire to become involved in social causes.

My child was most focused on . . .	My child has wings like . . .
☐ **Having someone help him**	**THE PROTÉGÉ.** Joe learns best in the presence of an expert. He dislikes learning by himself or in a large group. It is important that he be surrounded by those who will support and encourage him. *Flight Pattern:* a desire to learn from a mentor; affirmation and nurturing; the presence of a respected leader.
☐ **Putting something in order/ straightening up**	**THE ORGANIZER.** Ann believes that there is a place for everything. Disarray and a lack of organization confuse and annoy her. She is naturally driven to classify and organize everything in her path. *Flight Pattern:* the desire to put things in their place; to turn chaos into order; to develop and classify information systems.
☐ **Figuring something out**	**THE PROBLEM SOLVER.** Beth loves puzzles, mysteries, or anything that needs to be thought through and understood. She is invigorated by finding the piece that unlocks the mystery or the solution that solves the puzzle. *Flight Pattern:* a natural curiosity; time spent in thought; investigating and understanding.

My child was most focused on . . .	My child has wings like . . .
☐ **Making something match an idea**	**THE DREAMER.** Andy works in the cognitive realm. He enjoys thinking, exploring, and analyzing difficult concepts. It is important that the models and patterns in his mind become reality. *Flight Pattern:* understanding ideas; visual conceptualization; development of models and patterns.
☐ **Doing it his own way**	**THE FREE-SPIRIT.** Jason dislikes constraint, limitation, or boundaries. He is independent and self-directed. He likes to do things his way, according to his own agenda. *Flight Pattern:* independent thinking; avoidance of areas steeped in tradition, rules, and regulations; self-planning and regulation—a sense of control.
☐ **Being right**	**THE DISCERNER.** Mary is able to determine what needs to be done. She often acts on hunches and is usually right. She can read between the lines and implement an effective plan of action. *Flight Pattern:* discernment; right decisions; the confidence to follow her intuition.

My child was most focused on . . .	My child has wings like . . .
☐ **Having other people do what's right**	**THE JUSTICE.** James has a strong set of beliefs or convictions. When he believes in a cause he gives his full allegiance. It is important that he do what he believes is right. *Flight Pattern:* a sense of justice; evaluation of situations according to standards of right and wrong; connection between conviction and action.
☐ **Getting lots and lots of attention**	**THE STAR.** Rick likes it when all eyes are on him. He enjoys being the center of attention. Even in empty rooms he is drawn to podiums and stages. He needs to have others take note of his efforts. *Flight Pattern:* positions of prominence; a place in the spotlight; performances.
☐ **Having someone notice the work she's done**	**THE RESPONSE SEEKER.** Kathy thrives on having other people think well of her and of her work. She needs to have their approval and gauges her success or failure by the response of others. *Flight Pattern:* results; sensitivity to what others think.
☐ **Having someone notice him**	**THE UNIQUE.** Jerry enjoys standing out from the crowd. He likes to be recognized and highly regarded, but most of all he likes feeling different and special. *Flight Pattern:* positions of visibility; distinctiveness.

My child was most focused on . . .	My child has wings like . . .
☐ **Overcoming a challenge or an obstacle**	**THE PREVAILER.** John is driven to overcome difficult tasks or to triumph over trouble. He becomes bored when there are no obstacles to overcome. *Flight Pattern:* the pursuit of challenge; partaking in new situations; involvement in spite of difficult odds.
☐ **Discovering something new**	**THE EXPLORER.** Kenny loves to see what lies around every corner, discover new things, and experience new environments. He is not content with day-to-day routines; he needs to experience the unknown. *Flight Pattern:* discovery; avoidance of routine; trailblazing; pursuing the unknown.
☐ **Acquiring something**	**THE COLLECTOR.** Sarah loves to collect. She always is obtaining new items to add to existing collections. She is unable to throw things away because everything is a treasure. *Flight Pattern:* expanding the limits; always pursuing more of something—knowledge, skill, possessions, or experience.
☐ **Being responsible for something or somebody**	**THE RELIABLE.** Steve needs to do the right thing. He enjoys taking on duties and being trusted to fulfill his responsibilities. He is often seen in positions of authority. *Flight Pattern:* striving to win the trust of others; reliability; integrity; responsibility; leadership.

50

My child was most focused on . . .	My child has wings like . . .
☐ **Being important or necessary**	**THE INDISPENSABLE.** Debbie wants to occupy a central position. She enjoys making things happen. She likes having the sense that things would not have succeeded without her. ***Flight Pattern:*** a position in the center of activity; a need to make things happen; influential positions; a feeling that she is crucial.
☐ **Building something**	**THE CARPENTER.** Margaret needs to see growth and expansion. She finds reward in making things with her hands, seeing projects come to fruition. Once something is completed she will move on in search of a new area with potential for expansion. ***Flight Pattern:*** a need for an increase or gain; responsibility for growth; expansion of limits.
☐ **Doing exactly what someone expected**	**THE CONSCIENTIOUS.** Peter needs to have a sense that he has met the requirements of a given situation. If, upon completion of a task, he senses that he has missed a step or let someone down he will be discouraged and feel that he has failed. ***Flight Pattern:*** involvement with clearly stated objectives; all requirements must be known and met.

My child was most focused on . . .	My child has wings like . . .
☐ **Mastering something/ doing it perfectly**	**THE MASTER.** Greg is driven to produce the highest quality work. He is not content to be among the masses; he wants to be known as an expert, the top in his field. He puts forth unmatched effort to produce a perfect product. *Flight Pattern:* attention to detail; the pursuit of excellence; perfection; the search for new levels of achievement.
☐ **Creating something from nothing**	**THE CREATOR.** Teresa can turn a plain sheet of paper into a masterpiece. She has an unlimited source of creative ideas that require no external cues. She has a ready supply of fresh ideas and actively uses her imagination. *Flight Pattern:* resourcefulness; conceptualization; creativity; use of imagination; internal spark.
☐ **Doing it a better way/making something better**	**THE IMPROVER.** Donny has the ability to take the old and ineffective and make it better. He knows how to make an item increase in value. He finds satisfaction in developing things one step further, making them better than before. *Flight Pattern:* refinements; involvement with the inefficient; need for growth and increase.

My child was most focused on . . .	My child has wings like . . .
☐ **Having an adventure**	**THE ADVENTURER.** Leslie is not afraid to take risks. She often pursues areas that most people would avoid. She is bold and enterprising and dislikes routine. *Flight Pattern:* challenge; exploration; thrill and peril; enjoys uncertainty and the unknown.
☐ **Putting something together**	**THE DEVELOPER.** Mike is gifted at taking others' ideas and seeing them to fruition. He knows how to start the ball rolling, keep it on course, and get it to its proper destination. He may use creativity in the development process, but it is ignited by an external spark. *Flight Pattern:* an ability to complete the designs of others; planning and implementation; goals and guidelines.
☐ **Winning**	**THE WINNER.** Charlotte needs to win. She will become discouraged if she feels defeated. It is vital that she senses that she has won a battle, contest, or test of wills. *Flight Pattern:* a striving for success; planning and practice; a desire to be the best; competitiveness.

The clues to your child's strengths are found in what she did well in at school and in what happened when she didn't do so well; in what friends he has fun with and in why some kids his age he doesn't like at all; in circumstances that make you want to kiss her and in circumstances that make you want to clobber her.

53

See how important it is to describe your child's wings by using everyday words that describe everyday activities? Consider what might happen if a child is allowed to become an adult without guidance in how to make those strengths and abilities all work together as one set of wings. It's one reason I work with so many middle-aged adults who are still fluttering.

Exercise #2

Read the stories you've written about your child's activities. Can you see his or her strongest abilities? Begin to identify and develop an understanding of your child's wings by comparing the characteristics in the preceding list to the character traits of your child that you see beginning to emerge in your stories. Select two to four phrases that describe your child's truest joy.

5
▼

Look beyond your own expectations, frustrations, and disappointment to see what your child is really doing in a particular activity.

WHILE sitting in bleachers at my son's Little League game this summer I watched a little girl color a picture of a cartoon character. The girl was intent on her work, using dozens of different crayon colors on just one sleeve. All the colors were carefully blended together because she had figured out the trick of rubbing her index finger over the colors as she applied them. I enjoyed watching her. It's always fun to see a child focused so intently on her work, and this little one was busy.

But then her mother noticed what she was doing. "How many times have I told you that is not the way you color?" the woman scolded. "You are not staying in the lines. And how many sleeves have you seen that look like that?"

The woman then reached down and tore the page from her daughter's coloring book, crumpled it up, and tossed it into the garbage can at the end of the bleacher. Then she turned the girl's coloring book to a new page and began to show her how to color the "right" way.

Her expectations blinded her to a wonderful pair of creative wings her daughter was trying to unfold.

No doubt one of this mother's entries in the Good Kid Quotient would have been orderliness—and the ability to color within the lines.

This poor mom couldn't see what was right before her eyes.

A wonderfully creative daughter.

When you examine your child's stories, try to see what strength your child is exhibiting even if you don't like the outcome. View the action as if you were an unrelated bystander. If you can put aside the expectations you have for your child—and I know how hard this can be—you'll see that your children are consistently showing you their own unique set of wings.

✍ Exercise #3

In your stories, underline the "wings" your child was using. Keep looking for what your child is doing, good or bad, whether you agree with it or not, that is repeated from story to story. Use the new language from the preceding list.

6

Find out what your child liked the most about a particular project or activity.

WATCHING what a child does is often not enough to truly understand why he or she is doing it. So what do you do?

Ask.

"Great," I can hear you saying. "My child would never answer a question like that."

That's probably true. So you have to learn new ways of asking it. In effect, you have to let your children teach you the way to communicate about the things they love to do. And most of that communication will come down to one question . . . asked in many different ways.

THE GOLDEN QUESTION . . .

What did you like best about that?

If you learn clever ways to ask this one question—sometimes several questions for the same activity—out of your child's mouth will come the most significant insights about his or her own wings.

Amazing replies await you. You will enter another world and discover interests and agendas that you had no idea your child had.

Leah has decided to build a fort, and the neighborhood kids have been in your backyard all afternoon working on it. About the time it's finished you amble out to ask *the* question. You ask some warm-up questions and make comments to convince her that your interest is genuine, then you let it fly:

"What did you enjoy most about building the fort?"

"I dunno."

Rats, you think. You clear your throat and twirl the combination again.

"Well, what was the most fun?"

Click. Bingo. You hit paydirt. Out comes the answer: "It was fun making it look like the one I saw in a book."

Who knows *what* your child may say.

✗ *Getting other kids to help.*

✗ *Just building it.*

✗ *Figuring out how to build it.*

✗ *Getting it done by the time Dad got home.*

✗ *Hearing you say you liked it.*

You also may notice that she hasn't expressed any interest in playing with the fort. Her energy is already spraying off into other directions. This tells you something important too.

So you run back to the house and grab your notebook off the shelf. You've got terrific new material to add to your growing understanding of your child's wings, and you want to get it written down while it's still fresh.

In your enthusiasm, you've beaten me to Commandment #7. **57**

7

▼

Write down all the things you see and hear.

STARTING now, everything your child does when he or she is given freedom for self-expression, freedom to do what comes naturally, will be your teacher. Keep your workbook nearby and write, write, write.

TIPS
for unlocking a good story

❖ It may take several tries before you get a meaningful answer to the golden question. "I don't know" is generally the first reply. Don't let this frustrate you. Wait a few minutes and ask the question again in a different way. This gives the child time to think of an answer.

❖ Don't interpret. Don't ask any *why* questions; ask only *how* she did it or *what* he did.

❖ Consider yourself a journalist, an objective bystander writing a story about someone else's child.

❖ Keep pushing the story, thinking of new ways to ask the "golden question." When your child says what he or she liked about something, see if there is another verb in the response that you can use to to re-structure and re-ask the question.

Example:

"What did you like most about building the fort?"

"I liked making it look like the one in the picture."

"What did you like most about making it look like the one in the picture?

And so forth.

And once you know the look and the texture and the power of your child's natural abilities, you're ready to find your role in helping your child to fly.

Lisa's Story

All of Lisa's playmates were talking in sentences before Lisa had even said "Mama." The doctors weren't much help. The same people who told me the "only" way to feed my newborn were now telling me that if my child didn't talk by the end of the month she would have to be sent to special centers to be studied. Surely something was wrong, they said. Was it a hearing problem? Something wrong with her vocal cords? A learning disability? We knew Lisa had always been cautious in doing anything she couldn't do well and we figured the same applied to talking. Still, with all the other children speaking, and the doctors' concerns, we wondered. Then one day, she talked. I was elated. And within two days she went from perfectly pronounced words to full sentences. Nothing was wrong with Lisa. She just needed to be given the time and the freedom to do things in a manner that was comfortable to her.

Getting STARTED

#4 Recognize the ways in which children
exhibit fluttering. Here are five:
- ☞ Disobedience
- ☞ Poor grades
- ☞ Shyness
- ☞ Withdrawal
- ☞ Lying

#5 Know what makes a good story.
- ☞ Something your child *chose* to do
  (an activity or action)
- ☞ Something that your child had some
  control over
- ☞ Something that your child was able
  to do for as long as he or she wanted

61

Chapter Two

What Kind of Sky Does Your Child Need?

Finding the Places Where Your Child Soars

Be careful
what you throw
away.

—ELEANOR McMILLEN BROWN

WHEN A NEIGHBOR STOPPED by to tell the sad news that his wife had suffered a miscarriage the previous day, seven-year-old Cindy stood in the doorway and listened to Mr. Garber's story. Cindy's father noticed his daughter straining to overhear the conversation and was embarrassed at her seeming rudeness. He was about to scold her when she disappeared.

Shaken by the experience, the neighbor discussed the details for several more minutes with Cindy's father. Just as he was about to leave, Cindy reappeared. Dashing between her father and the neighbor, she pressed a piece of paper into the man's hand. Then she disappeared again.

Surprised, the neighbor looked at it, mumbled his thanks, and left.

Cindy's father, curious and a bit concerned about what Cindy had written on the paper, went looking for his daughter.

He found her in her room playing quietly. "May I come in?" he asked.

Cindy nodded, not looking up from the baby doll whose diaper she was changing.

"Did you hear what happened to Mr. Garber's wife, Cindy?"

"Yes."

"I noticed you gave Mr. Garber something before he left. Do you mind if I ask you what it was?"

Without speaking a word, Cindy stopped what she was doing and made a copy of the note she had given to

Mr. Garber. On the card, in sweet, childish crayon scrawl, was one word: "SORRY."

In telling me this story, the father was so overwhelmed with emotion at his daughter's compassion that he had to fight to control his voice, and his eyes filled with tears.

As Cindy's story illustrates, children have innate abilities that amaze even their parents. Unfortunately, these abilities often go unrecognized because parents misinterpret them. If Cindy's father had scolded his daughter for what he *thought* she was doing—being nosey—and made her leave the room, he might never have discovered her wings of compassion. If he had removed her from a situation that called for her special ability, both of them would have missed the opportunity to discover her surprising gift, and the neighbor would have been **66** denied a much-needed expression of compassion.

1

There are places where your child SOARS.

BY now you have noticed (if you've been recording your child's stories) how important environment is to his or her work and play. When I use the term *environment* I don't mean an atmosphere of love and acceptance. I mean something more specific. Because of the unique abilities your child was born to express, he or she moves with greater freedom and more enthusiasm in some places than in others.

Your unique, one-of-a-kind child is more comfortable in some places than in others.

Did Cindy seem out of place eavesdropping on a neighbor sharing his sorrow? Looking through our adult eyes, the answer is yes.

But in this instance, a roomful of trained people-helpers could not have responded more appropriately to the man's need at that moment than young Cindy did.

Think, however, what could have happened if her father had been a bit faster and had pushed her out of that seemingly inappropriate place. What if he had said, "Cindy, go back in your room. This is none of your business"?

Imagine the frustrated Cindy alone in her room, urgently needing to express her sympathy for the man but without opportunity to do so. She would have been like a caged sparrow flapping its wings until finally overcome by exhaustion.

But Cindy took flight before her father could lock her into that cage. Quietly she lifted off and went soaring to meet the need of her distressed neighbor. Then, just as quietly, she flew away.

Some places *stimulate* our children's wings into flight . . . Other places *inhibit* them.

Unknowingly, Cindy's neighbor created an important "place" for the seven-year-old. As he stood there talking about adult things, Cindy sensed his distress. Suddenly what she was doing in her own room wasn't as important as what she could do in another place. And nothing mattered except doing it, despite what her father might do or say.

When you and I recognize and steer our children toward the places where they are at their best, where they find joy in work and play, they will spread their wings and soar with little or no flapping.

And for every child, the places are different.

Megan, my youngest daughter, loves to play behind closed doors. She talks to herself and is content in her own world of imagination. Her older brother and sister have yet to ever close their doors (although I have considered nailing them shut a few times). Yet all three need me to understand and accept the places where they are most comfortable.

What might these be? Here are a few places where I have seen children SOAR . . .

Caring places

Diana loves helping at the Special Olympics track meet

and going with her Sunday school class to visit the nursing

home. She moves instinctively toward places where she can attend to the needs of others. Her parents' biggest concern is her ability to take care of herself before she takes care of everyone else.

Fast-paced places

Abigail enjoys the challenge of doing everything fast—even cleaning her room. Some people call her "intense." She moves from one activity to another and doesn't stay interested in one thing very long. Her parents dread summer because they can't find enough things to keep her busy.

Hands-off places

Jim has a huge DO NOT DISTURB sign on his door and a lock on his desk drawers. He needs space where no one bothers him and where he can keep all of his own stuff. He doesn't like to be smothered with instructions, or even hugs, and prefers to do things his own way, even if he makes mistakes. Jim's parents are frustrated with his keep-away attitude, sometimes to the point of being hurt by his brisk responses.

69

Creative places

In art class, Sarah knows immediately what to do with the
clay she is given. Coloring inside
the lines never occurs to her, nor
does using the normal colors for
anything. Her grass might be
green one day and periwinkle
blue the next. She always has an
idea in her head and works it
into whatever activity she is
involved in. She enjoys creating

and structuring her environment according to some inner
vision she has. Her mom worries that Sarah's teacher will not
appreciate Sarah's creativity and will stifle it.

Structured places

Dick likes to color within the lines and feels great when
people compliment him on how well he's done it. The best
way for his mom to get him to do his chores is to give him a
list. He does all his homework every night simply because it is
expected and is upset if his parents make him go to bed before
he completes every last page. He is frustrated when a "place"
has no clear guidelines or rules. His parents are often irritated
because Dick cannot start anything unless he has clear directions.

Interactive places

Vicki loves after-school activities that involve lots of kids.
She needs to feel that she is a part of the lives of others. She
not only plays with her door open, she seems lost when she is

by herself. She annoys her mother by following her around the house begging her to play.

New/versatile places

Chip loves it when his dad tries a new route even if they get lost. He is bored by the ordinary and is always searching for something new and exciting—whether it's a new super-hero or the latest electronic gizmo. He hates anything that is routine and avoids it whenever he can. And that includes his one major chore each week—taking out the garbage. He has missed it fourteen times in a row. But who's counting? Besides his mother and father, that is.

Free places

Janet likes to play in the sandbox. There she is her own boss and can rearrange things the way she likes them. She continually frustrates people who try to help her. Her parents

71

get tired of having her get angry whenever they tell her what to do.

Encouraging places

Bill likes to play on the volleyball team because his coach is always yelling support and is quick to tell him when he does something right. He loves to have people encourage him. He's easily discouraged when his mistakes receive more attention than his successes. His dad is concerned that even the slightest words of discipline hurt Bill.

Developmental places

Jeremiah loves his new woodshop class because he can get his hands into his work. He struggles when he is confined to a textbook and flourishes when he can get physically involved in a project. He loves to get his hands dirty. His parents are happy to know that  he loves building things, but the hammering is driving them up the wall.

Different places

Pammy likes to try out new ways of doing old tasks. She never walks the dog on the same route twice in one week. She spends a lot of time putting together different outfits to wear to school. Her mother wonders if Pammy will ever set the dinner table the same way two nights in row.

Adventurous places

Leon likes to be wherever a thrill is in the air. He once climbed to the top of a ski jump and sledded down by himself, almost breaking his neck. And he can't wait to do it again. Everyone thinks Leon is crazy. His parents fear he will kill himself before he is thirteen.

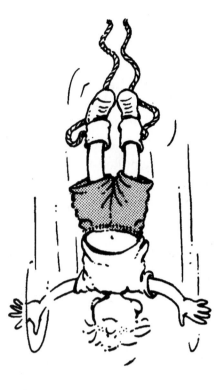

Challenging places

Ricky likes a challenge. He prefers "How fast can you run downstairs and turn off the light?" to "Ricky, will you please turn the lights off downstairs?" He loves it when people say he can't do something. His parents are tired of having to couch even the smallest requests as challenges to get Ricky to do them.

Scripted places

Katie loves to work behind closed doors and take on an identity other than her own. Whether her role is movie star, teacher, or mother, she never tires of being someone else. She plays any role that has a script to it. Mom lets Katie wear her old clothing and jewelry, but she draws the line when Katie

73

starts pulling new clothes from everyone's closets for her acting.

Places. There are all kinds of
them for all kinds of kids—all kinds
of skies for all kinds of birds. Can you
see them? Your child is naturally, sub-
consciuosly pulled toward some and
not others. And some of them puzzle
us . . . some even worry us.

 Exercise 1

Look at the stories you've written in your child's
workbook and ask yourself the following questions:
1. In what type of places did my child work or play
   most comfortably and naturally?
2. Which places are the most difficult to provide?
3. Which places am I the most fearful or disapproving
   of? Why?

2
▼

*Children naturally make their
way to the places where
they fly the best.*

SOMETIMES children thoroughly puzzle us. Think of one
action your child has done recently that you can't explain.

Maybe it's something she does all the time. Maybe it's something he's just begun doing or has only done once.

What can explain . . .

❖ The little girl who keeps turning around and talking to anyone who will listen?

❖ The little boy who copies his homework onto a new piece of paper so that it looks neat?

❖ The girl who puts her hand on mama's back while she is crying and soothes her with caring words?

❖ The eight-year-old who leaves the yard without permission and goes to the mall with some neighborhood children?

❖ The daughter who peeks into her mama's bedroom and tries to match what Mom is wearing?

These children are all doing what comes naturally to them, spreading their little wings in their own unique way. In fact, many go out of their way to find places to spread them. And that alone may explain a lot of unexplained behavior.

But there is good news. By noting the PLACES your son or daughter gravitates toward, you can predict what he or she might do. Then, instead of standing with brows furrowed, thoroughly befuddled, you can respond in a way that's right for you and for your child.

Your child's activity might *surprise* you . . . maybe even *confuse* you . . . but if you let it, it will definitely *inform* you.

If you are trying to get your child to function in an environment that is unnatural, he or she will automatically move away from it, no matter how much you force the issue.

How many times have you ushered your son into his messy bedroom with instructions to clean it up only to find him ten minutes later in another part of the house? How often have you ordered your daughter to finish her homework before getting out of her chair only to find her drawing cartoon characters all over her math paper when you checked on her ten minutes later?

Such behavior isn't necessarily outright rebellion. It may be a natural response to an unnatural environment. The "place" didn't feel right, especially if he is a messy kid or she is not a structured learner.

Some authorities would have you believe that such behavior demands discipline, that parents need to exert massive amounts of effort to train their children to perform well in every environment—no matter how unnatural or uncomfortable it may be for the child.

Although discipline is an important and serious topic, I suggest something very different in such situations. For now, simply understand this:

Children are always moving toward the place where their wings naturally unfold and take flight.

They are moving toward that place or not moving at all.
Sometimes it is a good place.
When it is, everyone is happy.
When it is not, there's trouble.

3

Parents can navigate their child toward the environment that is best-suited to his or her unique abilities.

CHOOSE the right "place" for the following kids:

✏ *Little boy Picasso*

EXPERT: "Your son is preoccupied with art. He needs to be more well-rounded."

Should you:

a. make him join a basketball team?
b. test him for a learning disability?
c. allow him to draw only on weekends?
d. buy him all the crayons he wants?

✏ *Little girl Florence Griffith-Joyner*

EXPERT: "Your daughter is always outside running with the boys. She needs to spend more time with girls her age."

Should you:

a. teach her to act like a lady?
b. make her wear dresses all day?
c. push her into a sewing class?
d. buy her the best running shoes you can find?

✏ *Little boy Edison*

EXPERT: "Your son is always playing with the lab equipment in science class. He needs to learn self-control."

Should you:

a. take him out of science until he learns self-control?

b. tell the teacher to make him sit in the back by himself?

c. suggest he be put in charge of all the lab equipment?

✏ *Little girl Streisand*

EXPERT: "Your daughter needs to learn cooperation. She refuses to sing the music the way it is written."

Should you:

a. allow the director to take her out of the musical and assign her to the stage crew until she can sing along with the rest of the choir?

b. sign her up for music reading lessons?

c. look for opportunities for her to sing solos.

The answers seem obvious, but when you're in the middle of any such situation they're anything but obvious.

Whether these famous-to-be children had someone to guide them into the right places, I don't know. But I'm guessing they did. Surely someone took the time to steer them into the environments where they worked and played the best.

Our son, Josh, works best in places where there is a challenge to overcome. So when his grade in English started to slip we took him to meet the honors English teacher at the high school he would attend the following year. That did it. The challenge to make honors English as a freshman was all he needed to bring his English grade back to an A.

Our daughter Megan spends hours with her dolls behind closed doors in her room. We have arranged for her to be the youngest nursery worker at our church. The first Sunday of each month, you can find our seven-year-old helping the nursery workers care for the babies. And she'll be smiling from ear to ear.

Talia, our eleven-year-old daughter, loves to be in a place where she can improve things. Two summers ago when we were buying eyeglasses for her brother, Talia moved around the shop putting frames away and straightening up. I whispered to the optometrist, "How would you like a volunteer to come in on Saturday mornings and do things like that for you?" So Talia may be the youngest optometrist's assistant in Illinois. She answers the phone, files, keeps the lab area straightened up, and is learning and loving it.

Nothing in these stories is extraordinary. We're just ordinary parents who are paying attention and enjoying the task of navigating rather than the frustration of enforcing.

You have the same power. You have the ability to navigate your child toward the absolute best environment by . . .

CHALLENGING
your child to spread his or her natural wings.

GUIDING
your child into situations best suited to the use of his or her abilities.

ARRANGING
the right place at the right time.

Do all parents do this? No. If they did, there would be fewer adults still fluttering at age forty.

Think what a difference it might have made in your own life if someone had guided you toward places best suited to your abilities. If you'd been given an opportunity rather than a reprimand. If you had been told what you *could* do rather than what you *couldn't* do. If you had developed confidence **80** rather than insecurity.

Perhaps many of us would not have the nagging feeling that we were designed to fly higher and farther and stronger . . .

Think about how difficult it is to deliver good results in a place where your own "wings" don't work well. Do you expect more from your child than from yourself?

4

Sometimes children need to keep their wings folded.

After all of this talk about places and abilities, there is one point that still needs to be made—and made hard. There are times and places when it is wrong for children to exercise their strengths and abilities. For example:

❖ a teenage girl who thrives in places where she can meet the needs of others begins to date a boy who complains that his physical needs are not being met.

❖ a teenage boy with a brand new driver's license who finds challenging circumstances invigorating goes to a party where he is challenged to take "just one drink" just before taking some friends for a spin.

81

❖ a pre-teen who likes to surround herself with
   beautiful things sees a gold chain that's been
   left setting out on a jewelry counter.

Each of these children is one "wing flex" away from dan-
ger. In moving to satisfy a need so natural that it seems to
demand no thought at all, our children may put their future,
even their life, in serious jeopardy. The wondrously strong and
energetic wings that enable our children to accomplish surprisingly good deeds sometimes carry them to places where they
ought not to be. At such moments, their unique abilities
become a terrifying, self-willed force that fights any hands
that seek to guide it.

What we have learned in pain through our own experiences of fluttering is what we need to communicate to our
children at such times: That sometimes a sky will look just
right, offering us the chance to spread our wings, to respond
to the inner call of our abilities—yet something about it can
be wrong. And the fall can be great and the damage severe.

We all know adults who never learned this discernment
in the call of the skies. Children can easily grow up to be
adults who still spread and flap their wings at every opportu-

nity without thought. Your own wings might have been badly bruised because you used your abilities at the wrong time in the wrong place. While we delight in watching our children SOAR in safe skies, we also have to teach them to keep their wings folded when the timing or the circumstances are not conducive to safe flight.

Maybe you don't have a baby boy Picasso or a little girl Streisand. But you have someone just as precious. Every child has abilities far beyond what he or she is usually allowed to discover. And with understanding and sensitivity you can provide an environment that will allow your child to develop his or her wings, test them, and learn when to use them and when not to.

Getting children into the right places and helping them avoid the wrong ones may be the most important work a parent will ever do.

Drew's Story

We loved playing with our toddler, Drew. It never occurred to us that he needed the company of kids his own age. When we took him to parks and placed him the church nursery he seemed more comfortable exploring on his own than he did playing with the other three-year-olds around him. But after our friends found out that we had decided not to put him in pre-school (a cardinal sin in their eyes) they told us that he needed to be with kids his own age. So we tried. Drew's first hour at play group was as confusing for him as it was for us. He spent all his time examining his new surroundings rather than playing on the gym equipment with the other kids. The instructor was certain Drew just needed more structure and kept pushing him back into the groups.   On the ride home Drew was so quiet and withdrawn that not even a short trip by the beach cheered him up. That night I lay in bed and wondered when I would learn to follow my own instincts with our child.

#6 Identify four of the places where your child works best. Post them in a place where you can be reminded of what they are.

#7 Navigate your child toward three places where he or she would work well—perhaps a hobby, an adventure, or a relationship. Use your imagination.

#8 Examine your child's classroom. How does that environment motivate or frustrate your child? Be prepared to defend and protect your child if necessary.

Chapter Three

What Is the Wind beneath Your Child's Wings?

Unleashing the Power that Keeps Your Child SOARING

He is well paid
that is well
satisfied.

—WILLIAM SHAKESPEARE

SOMETIMES PSYCHOLOGICAL JARGON keeps us from understanding what we really need to know. Fuzzy phrases like positive affirmation, self-esteem, self-perception, stroking, and a dozen others cause us to miss one very important factor of successful parenting:

Every child needs positive responses to his or her *work.*

When hugging your child have you ever felt as if you were transmitting energy straight into his soul? Did you know you can hug your child with words as well as with your arms?

Hugging your child with words

Once you recognize your child's unique abilities, and once you identify the environment best suited for the expression of those abilities, there is still another factor necessary for successful flight: the proper wind conditions to keep your child aloft.

The wind that keeps children in the air is their parents' positive responses to the use of the child's natural abilities. The more positive acknowledgement given, the more freedom children feel to use their wings, and the more they are used, the stronger they become.

89

Dear Mama,

I know I frustrate you sometimes.
I wish I knew what gets you mad.
I hardly ever think about what I do.

I just do stuff. And sometimes it's o.k.
but sometimes I get in trouble. A lot
of times I am really confused.

It seems like everyone only tells me what I
do wrong. Sometimes I feel like there must
be something wrong with me for so many
people to be yelling at me for so many
things.

All I know is I love when you tell me
something I did was good. It makes me
feel important. Makes me want to do
even more stuff that is good. Makes me
feel like someone understands me.
You know?

Your son,

Timmy

The right response evokes feelings of accomplishment and success and eagerness to try again. The wrong response evokes feelings of failure and fear of ever trying again.

Some of us grew up in environments where no one ever acknowledged what we did well. Most comments were connected to what we did wrong. But negative words are like salt on a bird's feathers. They are weights that keep children and adults alike earth-bound, afraid to flex for fear of being reproved.

That's what Timmy was trying to say in his note to his mother. If Timmy's mother could learn to uplift her son with words of reward, she would be amazed at his ability to soar.

"Fine," you say, "I do that. I tell my child I love her. I tell him he's special."

Terrific. Don't stop. Those words of affirmation are essential, foundational, and vital. But they are NOT words of reward. Here is where the psychological jargon sometimes gets in our way. In an attempt to build our child's self-esteem, we often mistake words of affirmation for words of reward.

The difference between affirmation and rewards

Affirmations are general, given on principle; they are hugs that provide comfort. Rewards are specific, given in recognition of accomplishment; they are hugs that inspire.

> **Affirmation,** *n., a statement of love that creates a climate of warmth and appreciation.*

> **Reward,** *n., a statement of fact that describes the quality and value of a child's work or play.*

Rewards may be verbal or physical. The verbal ones may be addressed directly to the child or spoken to a neighbor within earshot of the child.

In either case they relate to an activity your child has been involved in; they are statements that recognize the quality of his or her work or play.

Consider the following rewards and note how they differ from affirmations:

- ❖ You used wonderful colors on that drawing.
- ❖ You fixed the drawer so that it opens perfectly.
- ❖ This card you made for me made me cry.
- ❖ Wow! You finished every one of the chores on your list.
- ❖ I'm impressed that you did that job so fast and so well.
- ❖ I am going to put this clock you made up here so everyone can see it.

All these reward statements have one thing in common. Every one is connected to something the child did while using his or her natural abilities.

Now you try. Which of the following are affirmations and which are rewards? Put an ✖ by the affirmations, a ✔ by the rewards:

- ☐ I love you.
- ☐ You are important to me.
- ☐ You did a fine job dressing yourself today.
- ☐ You are a good brother.
- ☐ It was kind of you to help the neighbor take in her groceries.

☐ **You are my sweetheart.**

☐ **Good try.**

☐ **This picture is so colorful I'm going to put it over my desk.**

☐ **You learned that piece of music quickly!**

Do you see the difference?

The energizing effect of rewards

Rewards have an instant effect. And I do mean instant. Statements about the quality and value of what your son is attempting or your daughter is building provide the energy and enthusiasm necessary for them to SOAR.

Try it. Children worn out from work or play will react to words of reward as if you'd given them an energy transfusion.

When do you give these rewards?

Whenever a child does good work.

Look at the report card my daughter received from her fifth grade teacher. Unfortunately, the teacher used the place for making comments as an opportunity to point out Talia's one problem rather than to commend her for her many accomplishments. As a result, Talia received rebuke rather than praise, even though her grades were excellent. She came into the house crying over a wonderful report card. *That's* how powerful words are.

REPORT CARD

Science	
Spelling	A
Reading	A
Social Studies	A
Math	B
COMMENTS:	A

Talia needs to work on her talking in class.

93

Do you think Talia got back the energy she put into her good work? Granted, she may have needed to hear the comment about excessive talking, but she would have heard it much better if her scholastic achievements had been given their due reward. She deserved to hear both. And she will continue to soar in the skies of academia only if the winds of reward are at least as powerful as those of rebuke.

Who besides yourself needs to be rewarding your child? A teacher? A coach? Brothers and sisters? Grandparents? Are they doing so?

1

Look for opportunities to reward your child.

IF rewarding each other for good work came naturally we wouldn't be talking about it here. Many of you already understand the need to reward your child but find it difficult to remember to do so. It takes discipline. But remember, the most important rewards your child receives will come from *your* mouth. Be aware of every detail in your child's activity so that the rewards you give are real, reflecting something he or she has actually done. In other words, be sincere. Kids know the difference.

94

2

Reward your child consistently.

THAT means AT LEAST every week. Preferably every day. A once-in-a-while reward pattern will help neither you nor your child. As you discover the special rewards your child needs to stay aloft, you become the "keeper" of those rewards. You hold the power to motivate, inspire, and send your child soaring into the skies where he or she will fly the highest, the farthest, and the longest. How sad when rewards are held back or not given at all . . . and how weak and brittle unused wings can become.

3

Avoid "negative" rewards.

BE careful. You now possess the power to wound your child deeply.

- ❖ **Those colors don't go together.**
- ❖ **I should have fixed the drawer myself.**
- ❖ **The face on the clock you made is crooked.**

Negative words do more than rob you of the opportunity to infuse your child with enthusiasm. They actually squeeze energy from your child like a cider press squeezes juice from an apple; negative words leave your child limp and lifeless. We discourage our children in this way more than we think. Parents who heard mostly negative comments about themselves while growing up are particularly vulnerable to this behavior. **95**

4

Reward your child face-to-face.

Look at me when I am talking to you!" We've all said that when scolding our child. There's a reason. Something special happens when two people look at each other eye to eye. And something significant is sacrificed when you or your child turns away. How do you say "I love you" without looking at your child? Our eyes truly are the window of our souls. So when you reward your child, don't do it as he rushes through the kitchen or as she heads out the front door. Stop for a moment and face your child. Look into her eyes until you truly see her. Look into his eyes until your souls are connected. Then tell your child what he or she has done that is good and why it is good. Rewards given face-to-face are the most precious of all.

5

Reward your child's WORK.

KEEP the distinction clear between affirmation and rewards. Continue to affirm with loving words, but remember: rewards are essential because they are ALWAYS connected to WORK or PLAY, something your child actually did. Your attention to the details here can go a long way toward keeping your child in the air.

6

Display your child's work.

IN one home I visited the father pointed proudly to a display of his daughter's work arranged on a shelving unit the length of the entire hallway. As he pointed out to me the detail and color of several of the pieces, his daughter stood by

watching and listening, blissfully content. He said the most important thing they had ever done for their daughter was to create a space to show her work.

A shelf, a refrigerator door, a wall—displaying a child's work provides opportunities for meaningful rewards.

7

Schedule your child's rewards.

98 I F you keep a calendar, pencil in one or two times each week when you will reward your child. Keep track of things during the week that deserve commendation. Remember that the rewards you give will restore, encourage, refresh, and motivate your child to stronger, healthier patterns of flight.

Rewards are free, but for as many as we give and receive you would think they cost thousands of dollars each. Why do you think people are so stingy with them?

8

Keep it simple.

ONE last but extremely important tip: Be specific and sweetly simple. It takes only a few well-placed, touching words to keep that kid of yours flapping high and happy.

- ❖ Those colors you chose match perfectly.
- ❖ **That was a wise decision.**
- ❖ You sure did that fast!
- ❖ That woman appreciated you pushing her wheelchair.
- ❖ How did you figure out how to put that together without anyone telling you?
- ❖ **You did a wonderful job completing everything on that list.**
- ❖ How did you come up with such a creative idea?

❖ You picked up all your toys the first time I asked.

❖ You did so well I think I can trust you to do this.

❖ **I saw you go up to that new girl and say hi. That was really nice.**

❖ That's just like a mail-man would do it.

❖ I can't believe you pulled that off!

❖ I love the way you color-coordinated your socks in your drawer.

❖ Knives on the right, forks on the left. Perfect.

❖ Are you the one who left that candy on my pillow?

❖ **I think I can use that pencil-holder you made in school right here.**

Exercise #1

Choose an event or activity in which your child recently invested lots of his or her energy.

1. Write a new story noting the abilities your child used.

2. Use the story to help you figure out what reward he or she might appreciate.

3. Think of the perfect reward words that will express to your child your appreciation for his or her efforts. Then use them.

When rewards become traps

A lot of misbehavior occurs when children spread their wings at inappropriate times or in inappropriate places. And now a new piece to the puzzle: Rewards can come from inappropriate people. Just as there are dangerous "places," there are dangerous rewards.

Children naturally look for rewards. Rewards are the wind beneath their wings—wind that is necessary for staying aloft. And if you don't provide your child with that wind someone else will.

Your child wants to stay aloft. The temptation to fly on the wind of rewards from the wrong people or at the wrong time or in the wrong place is real and it is powerful. The overriding need for encouragement can cause a child to form damaging relationships and do unhealthy things. Sometimes even when you are offering better ones at home. It is less likely to happen, however, if you are rewarding your child at home. Properly rewarded children are better equipped to withstand ill-winds that threaten to push them off course.

Fill your child's wings with encouragement. Show him what he does well. Remind her a thousand times and then another thousand times that her abilities have value. Erase forever your child's need to have others provide this crucial dynamic.

Rewarding your child is a privilege. No one else will ever take your place if you fill this responsibility carefully.

Drew's Story

Drew had always loved playing with Legos. Ninety percent of his play time since he turned five had been spent building planes and space shuttles with the little plastic connecting blocks. He'd create and then he'd proudly show us the finished product. But then he suddenly stopped playing with them, and we wondered why.

We had always been careful to praise all his work and show our interest. What we didn't realize, however, was that every time we made him take apart his creations so he could make something else we were telling him that his efforts weren't worth saving. All the praise in the world was worthless to Drew because he needed to display his "trophies." All we saw was an ever-growing collection of useless inventions and the cost of continually buying a new set of Legos. He saw hours of hard work that he could show to others and play with himself. We were giving him verbal pats on the back but we were contradicting ourselves when we made him dismantle his work. What he needed more than our verbal affirmation was to have our actions match our words.

Getting STARTED

 # 9 Establish a reward time for each day. Use it to give your child rewards face to face.

#10 Find a place in your house where you can display your child's work.

#11 Find one significant person other than yourself who will take responsibility to reward your child for work well done.

Chapter Four

What Is Your Child's Flight Schedule?

Understanding How FAST and How LONG Your Child Can Fly

The ability to simplify means to eliminate the unnecessary so that the necessary may speak.

—HANS HOFMANN

**OU CAN PUSH AND PULL AND**
encourage and instruct and guide and
punish and cry and yank out every one of
the hairs on your head as you try to figure
out the best way to deal with your child.
But when you are done with all of this self-destructive
behavior your child will simply hop from the nest and be
about his or her business.

It doesn't make any difference how you *want* your child
to be. Your child is going to be what he or she is.

Children will always go about their business because their
business is imprinted on their little beings. And if you have figured out that truth, you're on your way to understanding this
truth, too:

The job of all parents is to find out the business of their children.

When your child's business is at odds with yours, things
go sideways at home. And your child's use of time is often at
the center of the storm.

Dozens of times a day we say to our children things like:

❖ You're working too slow.
❖ You're going too fast!
❖ Aren't you finished yet?

107

- ❖ Hurry up!
- ❖ How long do we have to wait?
- ❖ Can't you stay focused?
- ❖ Go on to the next one.
- ❖ Just get it done.
- ❖ Not until you're through!
- ❖ Don't stop yet!
- ❖ They'll be here in a minute.
- ❖ Isn't that due tomorrow?
- ❖ Why did you wait 'till the last second?
- ❖ Just grab something!

When we use these phrases we're trying desperately to keep the chaos swirling around us from carrying us and our families away. We just want things "fixed." We want the child who's doing poorly in school to get motivated, the one who's fighting with his sister to shape up, and the one whose bedroom is a federal disaster site to learn that cleanliness is next to godliness.

So in our spare time we read books like this because we have such a passion to see things work out right for our kids.

But in order to "fix" the problems, we must always—continually—keep another fundamental truth in the front of our minds. Before we say one of the oh-so-normal things listed above when chaos begins to swirl, we need to remind ourselves that . . . **109**

A child's use of time is a key factor in understanding his or her behavior.

And only by paying attention to it do we have a chance of fixing some of the things that seem to be broken.

Okay, back to the action . . .

TIME. In our home, there is no single issue that attracts as much attention as do matters related to time.

Children seldom have *our* focus, *our* sense of urgency, or *our* desire to see a task completed.

ALEX is seven years old. She loves to put things in order. Her mother asks her to straighten the living room. Alex straightens the bookcases for an hour and when she gets all the books in order, she leaves, ignoring the games and pillows on the floor that her mom meant for her to pick up and put away.

MATT is ten. He is at his best when he starts something. He usually has twenty or so uncompleted projects around the house. His parents are always tripping over things which are half done. They are mystified as to how Matt's energy can be so high one moment and so low the next. Is he just lazy, they wonder, or does he have a serious attention problem.

BILLY is eleven. Everything he does, he does at 180 miles per hour. He talks fast, walks fast, and lives fast. Anything that can't be done quickly doesn't deserve to be done at **111**

all seems to be Billy's motto. His parents are tired of receiving notes from the teacher about his shoddy work in school. Billy is smart enough. He just won't slow down long enough to do a good job on anything.

Beware of evaluating your child in situations where he or she has been told what to do. These settings often reveal what your child DOESN'T do well, but seldom reveal what your child DOES do well.

The three faces of TIME

Alex, Matt, and Billy all spend time at different paces, seeing different things, and doing some things better than others.

But actually, there is no such thing as time. You can't buy a bottle of it at the grocery store or wear it as a hairstyle. Time is simply a way of measuring movement and activity.

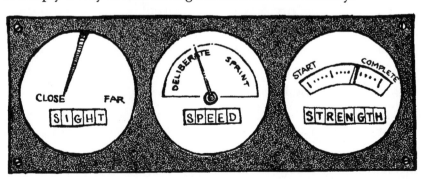

Dynamite in an hourglass, that's the power that lies in learning how your child uses time. Of course, seeing things the way your children see them isn't easy to do at first nor pleasant any time you attempt it. Let's face it, the simple fact is that you do few things the way your child does them. Trying to see the world through an offspring's eyes could drive even a Super Parent nuts. But it can also work wonders if you're willing to risk it.

Your child's use of time is probably quite different from yours. Understanding this concept can lead you to a celebration of your child's integrity and uniqueness!

113

1
SIGHT
▼

What your child SEES.

HAVE you been assuming that your child sees what you see? That is seldom the case. And the difference can affect every conversation and interaction you have together. Her vision and attention may be on things up *close* or *immediate*. You can't ever take for granted that you know what she is really seeing. You may see a mess of pillows and games on the floor of the living room while she sees books that are out of place in the bookshelf beyond.

What is going on is a question of *focus*. Your daughter may naturally focus attention on activities and situations and opportunities that she sees in great detail. Like the close-up lens on a camera, her eyes focus on a small area. Look at some of the things on which a little girl like Alex might focus her abilities and her attention:

What Alex Sees

❖ Whether her socks match
❖ Whether her shoes are lined up in her closet
❖ Wanting to finish reading a page before setting the table
❖ Stopping in the middle of a chore to bestow love on a cat

Or things she may *not* see . . .
❖ How much time her homework will take her
❖ The reality of a deadline until it is immediate
❖ Whether the *rest* of her room is cleaned up
❖ That she gets so involved in a project that it always takes *more* time than she thinks

On the other hand, a child like Matt may see faraway things more clearly.

He rearranges today's activities in light of what he sees coming. His attention to detail is not on the immediate but on the impending. His room may be messy like his sister's, but for a different reason. He is involved with something larger, something coming up, something he's building or planning. Like a zoom lens, he focuses on what is far off and actually reorders today's activities in anticipation of what he sees happening tomorrow. The consequences? A lot of stuff that needs to be taken care of today . . . isn't. Look at some of the things a child like Matt might focus on.

❖ Making sure he has enough spending money for next week's field trip.
❖ Planning his summer job in the middle of winter.
❖ Packing his suitcase for camp three days early (but only such things as swimgear and baseball glove, not underwear or towels).
❖ Asking at breakfast what's for dinner.

115

What Matt Sees

Or things he may not see . . .

❖ The importance of doing quality work on something small.

❖ A coat on the floor.

❖ A project he's started and left setting on the coffee table.

The reality is that your child probably is not locked into one focus or another (although some of you are looking right now at a child who is indeed just that). Most likely your child simply *leans* in one direction or the other. The leaning is best understood in the same way we have learned to understand everything else—by watching and examining what your child naturally does.

116   What you want to know is . . .

Does my child focus more clearly on things that are *close*, *far away*, or somewhere in the *middle*?

2
SPEED
▼

When your child is in flight, how quickly does he or she move?

THIS is what most parents are thinking of when they speak of time—how fast something gets done. Period. End of discussion. A child is either too fast or too slow. Too energetic or too lazy. Never quite what everyone would like. Too bad.

But like many adults, not every child enjoys working at the same speed as everyone else. Some adults work very quickly; some adults work very deliberately. Some children work very quickly; some children work very deliberately.

Deliberate fliers are . . .
❖ Precise
❖ Frustrated if they do not understand some-thing completely
❖ In need of plenty of time
❖ Good at processing every detail
❖ Thorough
❖ Not very good with deadlines

117

❖ Very careful
❖ Never sure when something is finished

Children who move deliberately will rearrange their flight pattern to get more time. They need more time to be more careful and thorough and to process every detail, making sure nothing is left undone. Every 't' must be crossed and every 'i' must be dotted. To urge them to hurry is to push them beyond their capabilities. They simply do not know HOW to hurry.

If your child is deliberate *and* close, he or she may spend an hour on a single page of spelling homework. Children like this need twice as many hours in a day to accomplish half of what needs to be done. Plenty of moms and dads experience this frustration themselves. Then there are sprinters.

Sprinters are . . .
❖ Expecting quick results
❖ Looking for fast action
❖ Waiting until the last minute
❖ Quick and dirty

❖ Out of breath
❖ Always in a hurry

For a sprinting child, finishing things or doing them right are not as important as doing things quickly—to keep from getting bored. In a world where many things need to be done carefully, life can be difficult for the sprinter.

Your child is probably somewhere between these two extremes, moving slowly sometimes and very fast at others. Some children, however, may move fast or slow all the time. In all cases, the speed of their movement tells you something about how and where they will fly most successfully. Your job as a mom or dad is to help them balance what they do naturally with the acquired discipline to accomplish what needs to be done.

3
STRENGTH
▼

When does your child have the most energy to use his or her abilities? When are your child's wings the strongest?

HERE is that word again—WHEN. The question continues to be not IF your child does what he should, but WHEN do you finally see results? WHEN will my child want to clean up his room, work on her homework, do his chores, work on that science project. When?

Like the other two hands of time, this one has two features of its own. Some children like to start things. Some children like to finish things. And a whole lot of children live somewhere in **119** the middle, always landing somewhere between starting and completing what is around them . . . in their own good time.

The explanation for the pace at which your child moves is surprisingly simple—and so is the practical application.

It's a matter of changing our expectations for our children and changing the way we speak to our children about their use of time. For example:

Instead of saying "She never finishes anything," you can say "She enjoys starting things."

Instead of saying "He won't start anything on his own," you can say "He enjoys completing things that are already started."

Remember, a child doesn't ordinarily do things simply to frustrate you or make you mad. Children act in accord with their natural patterns of flight. It is only when a child is flying in the wrong situations, disrupting the patterns established to keep order in the household or classroom, or when the child is inconveniencing others that his or her flight needs to be controlled.

Remember Alex and Matt and Billy.

Alex is "close," seeing only the detail of the messy bookshelf. Matt likes to start stuff. Billy is a sprinter. Nothing wrong with any of these, is there? But their parents have boxes of stories telling of times when those abilities have caused all kinds of difficulties.

Your child is speaking

Your child's use of time will communicate to you if you know what to watch for and know how to interpret what you see. One of the most important contributions parents can make in the lives of their children is to help them understand their own flight pattern, its advantages and disadvantages, and to train them in the necessary and correct use of time.

Drew's Story

Drew was excited about school; enjoying the classroom came naturally to him and he felt successful. We were shocked when he came into our room sobbing one night and telling us that he hated school. "No one likes me," he cried. Determined to figure out what was wrong, I volunteered to help out in his class once a week. The problem was evident immediately. It wasn't that the children didn't like Drew; they just didn't notice him. Most of them rushed through their work to get to play time. Drew took his time, perfecting each detail. By the time he was done, they were so immersed in their play time that they didn't see that he was waiting to be invited to join in.

#12 Make a weekly schedule of things that need to happen at your house at certain times. For example: the garbage has to be at the curb on Monday morning; everyone has to be ready to leave for church by 9:30 on Sunday morning. Where do the difficulties arise? How does each family member's own concept of time contribute to the problems? What can you do to help your child effectively use his or her time WITHOUT placing unrealistic expectations on your child?

#13 Is your child a deliberate flier or a sprinter? Choose three projects for your child to complete this week that can be done at his or her natural pace.

Chapter Five

Who's in the Flock Your Child Flies With?

Understanding How Your Child Works with Others

The art of
being wise is
the art of
knowing what
to overlook.

—WILLIAM JAMES

**O**NE SUNNY DAY ANN SENT HER SON, Sammy, out the back door to play with some neighborhood children on their backyard swingset. But Sammy, instead of making a beeline for the swings as his mom had anticipated, went to the sandbox where he began to dig quietly by himself. Ann stood in the doorway trying to decide what to make of the situation. Should she . . .

- ☐ take Sammy by the hand and walk him over to the other children.
- ☐ make an appointment with a child psychologist specializing in socially-maladjusted children.
- ☐ run for her copy of *Born to FLY!*
- ☐ make a mental note of what she witnessed and go on about her day.

Art is not about things as they are, someone once said, but about things as they matter. Have you ever thought of your child as a living, breathing work of heavenly art? Your challenge as you try to get that work of art ready for public display is to sort out the things that matter from things that simply are they way they are.

The truth of the matter is . . . "The language of truth is simple." —Seneca

125

The daily realities of messy rooms and squabbling siblings coupled with your own hopes and expectations for your child make it difficult indeed to pluck out the things that really matter. But learning to see those details will help you understand what a remarkable thing God has done in creating your child in his image.

So Sammy's decision to go to the solitary sandbox instead of the populated swingset is very important. Why? Because it gives his parents an indication of how Sammy works with people.

Just as different types of birds fly in flocks of varying sizes and for differing purposes, so people (including your child) work with others in various ways.

Unfortunately, few things about our children are as misunderstood as this truth. Entire school systems have trouble accommodating the wide range of people-style strengths children possess. Many teachers and parents alike never discover how a particular child interacts with others and what that interaction style reveals.

When I was growing up I had little interest in actually doing things. I had much more energy for finding the right people to get things done for me. When asked to wash the car, for example, I would find other kids who would enjoy washing the car (that definitely was a challenge). Unfortunately, this unusual work ethic of mine meant that a lot of jobs around our house were left undone. My parents might have concluded that my need "to find the right people" was not simply little Tommy's "informative childhood action" but a pain in the neck.

The truth, though, was that my behavior in this area was one of those things that mattered—it spoke volumes about my ability and need to relate to others—for good or bad. And if my parents had known how my "people-ability" worked, they probably could have figured out a way to get relief from the "neck pain" Tommy gave them.

QUESTION

What kind of flock does your child fly in

and how does he or she interact with

others in the flock?

Answer this question and you are well on your way to seeing (and coping with) your child's "people-ability."

Four formations of flight

Each of the FOUR primary ways in which children work with other people contains some of the truth already discussed.

1

FLYING SOLO
Children who fly solo don't require any exterior formation.

SOLO-FLYERS are concerned about their own work and their own effort. If they look up from their work to pay attention to what is happening around them, they begin to flutter.

Sammy enjoyed flying solo. Left alone, he was more interested in what he was doing than in the people and activities around him.

127

Nothing wrong with that. However, such a skill is seldom considered beneficial in our sociable society. In fact, some parents have been taught that flying solo is anything but good. That idea is not only a myth, it's also debilitating because flying solo is the only way some children (and adults) *can* fly.

Friendly Skies
Times when solo flying IS appreciated . . .

* a particular task is assigned

* work needs to be done alone

* the child is expected to entertain himself or herself

Unfriendly Skies
Times when solo flying is NOT appreciated . . .

✳ other children are playing nearby
✳ others want interaction
✳ someone wants to give input into the child's
work

When Sammy chose the sandbox over the swingset, his
mother realized that Sammy preferred to play alone. He
showed no interest in interacting with the others. He didn't
even acknowledge that they were in the same yard. His
mother had to decide whether to allow Sammy to soar on his
strongest wings or to use the opportunity to teach him some
necessary social skills.

Sammy may never interact especially well with others,
but his mother knows that he will need certain basic communication skills to get through life without major frustration.
And by noticing what matters she learned that the things
Sammy always will do *best* are the things he does *alone*.

Is your child a solo-flyer?

✳ Does she prefer working by herself or with
other people?
✳ Does he often play in his room with the door
closed?
✳ Does she often leave behind projects/work
that she has done herself?
✳ Does he prefer to play with his own toys
rather than share them with others?

✳ Is she not as easy to hug as some other children?

✳ When he has a friend over, do they play for long periods of time in silence, focusing all of their energy on individual activities?

2

FLIGHT LEADER
Children who are flight leaders have their own idea of where the flock should go.

ONE spring afternoon Jeff sent his little girl Katie outside to play with some of the neighborhood kids. After only a few minutes he heard arguing. He looked outside and saw his daughter giving orders to all the other children.

130

Should he . . .

☐ Bring Katie inside and spank her.

☐ Remind her for the thousandth time that she should not tell people what to do.

☐ Run for his dog-eared copy of *Born to FLY!*

☐ In one breath thank God for the marvelous way he designed Katie and in the other breath pray silently for the strength to manage her properly.

Some children, like some adults, naturally assume authority when they are around other people. Rather than being focused on the work they do individually, their best work involves directing other people. For instance, their work includes . . .

✷ getting people to change their minds

✷ getting people to respond

✷ motivating people

✷ making people laugh

✷ getting peoples' attention

✷ telling people what to do

✷ telling people what they did wrong

Katie is frustrated because, at her age, there are so few opportunities for her to be in charge of people. She would love to direct people all day long, but whenever she tries she gets into trouble. This causes quite a dilemma. Whenever Katie tries exercising her wings she receives more reprimands than rewards.

Her best activities in school are things like speaking to the class or leading a group activity. She detests sitting by herself behind a desk and she learns very little when she is working alone. But watch what she absorbs when she is able to stand in front of the class and help teach the very same material! **131**

Friendly Skies
Times when formation leaders ARE appreciated . . .

✷ someone needs to be convinced about something
✷ a group needs direction
✷ a part in a play needs someone to perform it

Unfriendly Skies
Times when formation leaders are NOT appreciated . . .

✷ other people want to do what THEY want to do
✷ the parent tells the child what to do and the child argues
✷ the child is expected to produce results ALONE rather than by influencing other people.

Is your child a flight leader?

☐ Does she take charge around other people?
☐ Do you often find yourself arguing with him about how something should be done even when you know he doesn't have the faintest idea what he is talking about?
☐ Does she get into a lot of fights with her friends?
☐ Does he enjoy bossing other kids?

Some teachers don't appreciate (or even notice) how children interact with others. Prepare to describe your child's "people-abilities" at your next conference with your child's teacher.

3

TIGHT-FORMATION FLYER
Children who fly in a tight formation use other people as a border for their activity.

JASON'S mom pushed him gently out the back door to play. He stood alone for a moment until he heard the sounds of children playing across the street. He ran over to the crowd and stood watching all the activity for several minutes. Finally someone asked him to make mudpies, and Jason rolled up his sleeves and dug right in. Some children use people (not in any bad sense) to define where they should be and what they should be doing.

Who is missing from the following list?

1. **pitcher**
2. **catcher**

133

3. **first baseman**

4. **second baseman**

5. _____

6. **third baseman**

7. **left fielder**

8. **center fielder**

9. **right fielder**

The missing shortstop in the team above needs eight other players to play ball. A ballerina needs an orchestra, supporting dancers, and an audience. And your child may need a friend who points to an empty swing and says, "Come play with me."

Some children need a group to help them define their place. While the children in our first two examples either worked alone or influenced the work of other people, a child with this "people-ability" allows the flock to determine what he or she does.

Friendly Skies
Times when tight-formation flying IS appreciated . . .

* ✳ when teamwork is important
* ✳ when there is a script to follow
* ✳ when someone needs to work closely with another

Unfriendly Skies
Times when tight-formation flying is NOT appreciated . . .

* ✳ an activity has no guidelines
* ✳ the child is expected to start alone and work alone
* ✳ the child is expected to lead the flock

Parents should pay particular attention to children who are dependent on a flock. Their lack of social initiative should not be confused with shyness, self-consciousness, or laziness. They simply need an opportunity or an invitation to join other individuals busy at work. Their "people-ability" is just as important as the others. A baseball team and a ballet troupe need every participant to perform. Teams have coaches and ballets have directors to bring out the best in every member of the group.

135

Is your child a tight-formation flyer?

- ☐ Does he enjoy working on something with someone else?
- ☐ Does she love being asked to do something? (I have a daughter who LOVES being asked to do something, so sometimes I ask her to put a deck of cards in order for me. And she *enjoys* doing it!)
- ☐ Does he get upset when his birthday gift for a friend is not as well received as some other gifts?
- ☐ Does she hesitate to move toward someone unless invited?

 **Exercise #1**

Think of a few of the problem situations around home that keep recurring (e.g., late homework or chores left undone). Can you find any people clues as to why the work isn't getting done? Jot them down.

4
▼

FLIGHT MANAGER
Children who are flight managers enjoy organizing and positioning those around them.

TOMMY has just been told to wash the car. (Uh-oh. Sounds like me again.) An hour later his dad looks out the window and sees every other kid on the block squealing and squirting each other as they rub his car clean, but not Tommy. Tommy is walking around talking with the kids and handing out buckets and rags.

Should his dad . . .

☐ Send the kids home and tell Tommy to wash the car by himself?

☐ Ask the kids if they do lawns too?

☐ Throw *Born to FLY!* in the garbage?

☐ Admire Tommy's extraordinary ability to mobilize other people and manage their activity?

Children who are flight managers are interested in organizing and positioning those around them.

In God's amazing scheme of creation, one thing is very clear. He never intended that people operate strictly on their own. His design is a complex blend of individual bursts of energy all coming together within his divine plan.

And sprinkled here and there are individuals who have a natural ability to organize and position all the energy we recognize as human personalities. They are the flight managers, the navigators. They make sure each person is in the right place at

the right time so the group can do its best. Like the flight leader, their best work involves the movements and directions of other people, but instead of getting people's attention or telling them what to do and how to do it, these little jewels simply make sure that each person is doing what is necessary to get the job done best.

So children who manage the flock have an interest in positioning people in the right places to get good results. The biggest problem these little ones face is the scarcity of opportunities to practice at a young age. Most of what is required from children comes from their own efforts, not from their ability to manage others. These children often hear a barrage of language describing what they *don't* do rather than encouraging them in what they *do* do and suggesting what else they *could* do. Often they hear . . .

Do it yourself!

Quit trying to make her help you!

Why are you so lazy?

Why won't you ever do anything by yourself?

Leave him alone!

Why didn't you help him do it?

Quit trying to bribe him to do your work.

I said that was your job!

Little Tommy got used to hearing those kinds of responses rather than the sweet music of: "Nice job getting the car washed! I was sure impressed at how many children you got involved and how much fun they were having. And you even made sure they had enough rags and buckets. Good work."

138   "Work?" What work? Why, managing the flock, of course.

Friendly Skies
Times when a flight manager IS appreciated . . .

✳ people need to be organized
✳ there is a job bigger than one person can handle
✳ new people are coming on the scene

Unfriendly Skies
Times when a flight manager is NOT appreciated . . .

✳ there is no need for a manager
✳ the child is expected to produce his or her own work
✳ an inexperienced or selfish leader makes unrealistic expectations

Children who have managing abilities are some of our most precious resources. We need to identify these little ones and give them opportunities to develop their wings.

One of my daughters, the same one who loves to take care of others, works with people in this way. At seven years of age, however, she can't find many situations that require her management skills.

But one night when I was tucking her into bed she asked softly, "Daddy, how are the children going to get back from the nursing home they are visiting on Sunday morning? Maybe we should get a bus for them."

139

Amazing. A seven-year-old making sure everything goes smoothly for the people involved in an activity.

Is your child a flight manager?

- ☐ Does she enjoy getting other people involved?
- ☐ Does he avoid winning a game if someone else has to lose?
- ☐ Does she anticipate what someone needs in order to do a good job?
- ☐ Does he have a particularly soft heart and is easily discouraged by stern words?

What about you? Do you fly solo? Do you lead the flock? Do you fly in formation? Do you manage the flight? Understanding how you relate to people will help you better understand your child.

Who is in your child's flock?

What kind of people surround your child? Look at them closely and answer this question: Does your child need people to . . .

- ☐ copy?
- ☐ be a part of?
- ☐ teach?
- ☐ manage?
- ☐ influence?
- ☐ coach?
- ☐ question?
- ☐ give advice to?

- ☐ lead?
- ☐ manage?
- ☐ mediate?
- ☐ correct?
- ☐ invite him or her to action?
- ☐ be an audience?
- ☐ compare to?
- ☐ organize?
- ☐ provide requirements?

As a parent, your responsibility is to strategically involve your child with the people who will help him or her soar at the right times and in the right direction.

Remember, one way or another, with or without your help, children find people who help them fly higher. Without your guidance—and sometimes even with it—your child may fill the right "people slots" with the wrong types of people.

Be careful.

Analyze the people around your child and then nudge your child toward those who will help him or her soar in the right direction.

And then, when needed, carefully choose opportunities to teach your child people skills that don't necessarily come naturally but are still necessary to know.

Drew's Story

*It's funny how different two brothers can be. Matthew finds a sense of satisfaction in being a helper; he wants to be in the trenches right alongside us, doing his part. Drew, on the other hand, has set opinions as to **what** should be done, **who** should do it, and **how** it should be done.*

We trimmed the trees recently. Matt, with a smile on his face and a twinkle in his eye, grabbed a saw and trimmed the limbs we had cut down.

But not Drew. He walked around with his hands on his hips telling his grandpa the right way to do it. When we told him to bundle the loose branches, he recruited a kid from the neighbor-hood to do it instead. He got the job done without lifting a finger—what a kid.

Getting STARTED

#14 Write stories about three situations that have helped you get a fix on the way your child works with other people. Don't be confused if he or she seems to have more than one ability. Some children have several. My daughter, for example, is primarily a flight manager, but when she is not in a place to practice this ability she works well in tight-formation situations.

#15 What people does your child need to help him or her fly well? Look at the preceding list and select the three most important people in your child's life.

#16 Find someone to explain your new understanding to.

Chapter Six

Born to Fly,
but Grounded!

Dusting off Discipline and Helping Your
Child Find the Right Skies

Knowledge is the antidote to fear.

—RALPH WALDO EMERSON

**ISCIPLINE. Exactly what is it?**

1. **Punishment to fit the crime.**
2. **My way or the highway.**
3. **Training in the way a child should go.**
4. **All of the above.**
5. **I'm not sure, but I know when I have to use it.**

Which would you choose?

Someone once said that all of life is a multiple choice question—everything's just a darn good guess.

Whatever shade of meaning we attach to the word *discipline*, it's powerful stuff. And many tragic mistakes have been made in the name of it. If it were easily understood and easily taught, much of the abuse that occurs under the label of discipline could be eliminated. But it is not easy. Discipline is more than a whipping in the woodshed or an evening without dinner. And it may be the most important area parents control in their relationships with their children.

And yet many of us get it all wrong, so wrong that we hurt instead of help. What do I mean?

By now, you've taught yourself to view almost everything else about your child from a new perspective. Now let's take a good look, a revealing look, at what discipline must be if we are to keep from harming our children's wings when they flutter and from damaging our fragile relationships with our children in the process.

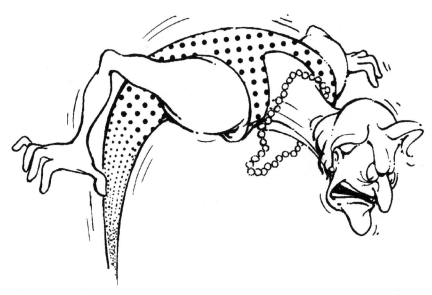

Five things discipline is NOT

Recall the last time you were in line at the check-out counter in the grocery store and the parent ahead of you was trying to control an unruly child. Which of the following terms would you use to describe the parent's response?

Angry

Excessive

Loud

Abusive

Degrading

Now recall the last time your child acted up at home. How did YOU respond? Be honest. Is the answer above?

One truth from this book that you can take straight to the

bank is this:

NONE of the words in the above list belong in the same sentence with the word *DISCIPLINE.*

I know, I know. You're only human. Parents use that excuse a lot, and with a perfect right, I admit. But there are some areas of parenthood that don't allow for *near*-perfection. They're way too important. And discipline is one of them. So if any of the above words are in your definition of discipline, now is the time to update your dictionary.

Breaking your own rules

Pie in the sky, your job is not. Being a parent is hours upon days upon weeks upon years of having little people running around doing things you don't want done, making mistakes, spilling milk, wasting your time, misbehaving, driving you to the point of momentary insanity. Believe me, I know!

THIS **WILL** BE ON THE TEST

Discipline, n., the activity of rearing healthy children through guidance and correction in the use of their natural abilities.

149

I also know that we get angry and frustrated and irritated and depressed and wild and nuts and sad and mad and lonely, and that sometimes we yell and scream and hit and allow all sorts of unpleasant things to come between us and our kids.

All under the guise of discipline

Since our use of discipline normally occurs during periods of out-of-control and inappropriate behavior, it is easy to understand why anger and frustration are frequently attached to it. But those all-too-human responses are not part of true discipline.

So then what is? We're getting to that, but first let me warn you: You may have to break your own rules about discipline. You may have to add some things to your understanding and remove some other things. You may have to change the way you think. You may even have to throw away hand-me-down concepts from your parents and friends if you want your child to fly high and strong and far.

Many behavioral problems fall into one of the following three categories. By determining which is which you can avoid knee-jerk reactions and inappropriate and ineffective discipline.

1

THE LABORATORY OF LIFE

SUZY spills her milk. Don't confuse this random behavior with serious stuff. Mistakes happen. Life is messy. Trial and error is a legitimate method of learning. Milk gets spilled no matter how careful a child is.

150

2
▼

WRONG PLACES

DONNY gets a C on a test. Why? Does it have anything to do with his style of learning? Is discipline called for—or something else? Maybe he needs help instead.

3
▼

DELIBERATE ACTION

 Jennifer tells her mother she's going to a youth group activity but goes instead to a party at a friend's house. There's no mistake here. Jennifer has made a choice. With or without thinking, she has spread her wings and is flying in the wrong direction. Without proper correction, her chances for personal injury and eventual destruction are great.

So you act. Keeping in mind the **five things discipline is not.**

151

To discipline or not to discipline?

Keeping in mind the three categories discussed above, which of the following situations call for discipline (**D**)? Which need only a simple word of correction (**C**)? And which need no comment at all (**NC**)?

D	C	NC	
☐	☐	☐	a spilled glass of milk
☐	☐	☐	a C on a report card
☐	☐	☐	taking someone's money without asking
☐	☐	☐	not eating vegetables
☐	☐	☐	a messy room
☐	☐	☐	unfinished chores

D	C	NC	
☐	☐	☐	an F on a report card
☐	☐	☐	talking back to a parent
☐	☐	☐	talking back to a peanut (just checking to see if you're paying attention)
☐	☐	☐	interrupting an adult
☐	☐	☐	hitting a brother
☐	☐	☐	leaving the yard without asking
☐	☐	☐	lying about eating a cookie

Ten things discipline IS

Copy the following ten things onto a piece of paper and put it on your refrigerator where you will see it several times every day (or snip the page designed for this activity from your workbook and display it). Read the list every day to remind yourself to **think before you act.**

1

Discipline is CORRECTIVE

DISCIPLINE shows your child *how* to fly. If he is flying upside down, it shows him how to right himself. If she is flying in the wrong direction, it shows her how to turn around and head the other way. Discipline always always makes it easier for the child to make the right decision the next time he or she is in a similar situation.

153

2

Discipline is LOVING

IF you want to get angry, go ahead. Just don't do it in the presence of your child. When you're wearing your disciplinarian cap, you must show your child a loving spirit. Wounds cut deep when anger is the emotion of the moment. Most of us remember at least a few childhood moments of parental anger as if they were etched on our psyche.

3

Discipline is SENSITIVE

YOU are like a pilot training a new recruit how to fly. You are keenly aware of how well your new student is doing, and you are careful to give her just the amount of instruction she is capable of hearing.

4

Discipline is FORCEFUL

YOU must be direct, your words pointing out clearly the proper behavior. Don't be apologetic.

5

Discipline is UNCOMPROMISING

MAKE sure your position is right. Beware of situations that are a matter of opinion. Many parents lost the effective use of discipline in the sixties and seventies by arguing over issues of hair length and dress. Remember?

6

Discipline is WISE

BE thoughtful in your movements and speech. Encourage yourself to think before you act. Remember what we said about discipline: It causes us to think of things outside ourselves. ***Discipline yourself*** before you act; think about the consequences of the disciplinary action you're considering. Wise words and careful corrections will do well for your child. And for you.

7

Discipline is APPROPRIATE

ALWAYS keep the discipline connected to the behavior. If consequences are involved, make sure they fit the misbehavior. Just because you are frustrated or angry doesn't mean it is right to swat your child to correct his or her behavior.

155

8

Discipline is QUIET

THE best discipline is not accompanied by loud voices. Forget any excuses for yelling. There are no valid ones. We never have a good reason for it, even though we've all been guilty of doing it.

9

Discipline is PRIVATE

EVEN though most misbehavior happens in front of others, your discipline should be behind closed doors. Enough said.

10

Discipline is PHYSICAL

WHETHER or not a spanking is a part of the punishment, make sure to hug and hold your child sometime during the discipline. Remember, discipline is for your child's *good,* to correct an inappropriate use of his or her wings. If you are angry, don't address the situation until you have collected yourself. If you are unable to hug your child and be loving, this is probably not a good moment to correct his or her behavior.

Name three things your child does that make you angry. Are they mistakes in the laboratory of life, actions done in the wrong places or at the wrong time, or deliberate choices? What is the best way to handle them?

Relaxed . . . and in control?

Yesterday my wife and the mother of two out-of-control children left the grocery store at the same time and walked to

157

the parking lot. Their eyes met as the woman was putting her groceries into the trunk of her car with one hand and swatting her kid with the other. She looked at Debbie in disbelief because our children were walking quietly by Debbie's side, each carefully holding a bag filled with groceries, their socks pulled up and their hair neatly combed. Debbie was in complete control.

HA! Pure fantasy.

But don't expect me to believe that you haven't had the same one.

If control is what you want, you need to find another book. But if you want to help your kids fly right, to become the best they can be, and feel in control of the discipline skills that will help them do so, here are five tips.

Mastering discipline—five tips

Know yourself and your child.

PARENTS who know themselves and their children don't fear their child's fluttering. For example, if you understand that you are the type of person who likes things in order, you will be on guard against being overly sensitive to your daughter's messy room. And if you understand that your son likes to acquire things, you will watch carefully what he does with other people's possessions.

But the understanding must go both ways. If parents understand themselves and not their child, they will lose ground in their battle to straighten their child's flight.

✍ Exercise #1

Write the answers to the following questions in your workbook or on a separate sheet of paper.

1. Do you understand how YOU fly?
2. Do you understand how your child flies?
3. What statement best describes the way you and your child are alike?
4. What statement best describes the way in which you and your child are different?

A few weeks ago I was following my son around the house needling him about something. I enjoy getting a response from people and I was certainly getting one from him. I followed him through the family room, past my wife, and into his bedroom, poking fun and razzing him all the way. I knew he was getting angry, but I didn't stop. Finally he yelled at me to leave him alone and slammed the door in my face.

Now I had a problem. He had raised his voice to his father and slammed the door to his room, two things we never allow the children to do. As I was standing nose to nose with the slammed door, I was thinking about how I was going to handle this. I looked over to Debbie who just sat there shaking her head.

"Provoke not your children to wrath," she quoted a little too piously, as if this wasn't the first time the scripture had popped into her mind.

Kids aren't the only ones who have to be corrected. Parents sometimes need it too. Knowing I'd been wrong, I quietly opened Josh's door and apologized for making him angry. I knew my son well enough to know he would forgive me, and he did. But I also knew that he knew that his response had been unacceptable. So after admitting that I started it, I still pointed out his wrong response, which he admitted. And so I was able to forgive my child as well as show him that I can accept responsibility when I'm wrong, a good lesson for both of us. **159**

2

Win your battles in secret.

A CLEVER parent heads off problems before others even know they are problems. Parents get little credit for making such decisions, though, because those battles are won in private. Outsiders know nothing of them. Excellent parenting is not fighting and conquering your child so everyone will say, "Well done."

True excellence is being aware of your child's intentions ahead of time so you can correct them before they occur. And that takes courage and wisdom of the quiet, insightful kind.

✍️ Exercise #2

You're reading this book late at night. The kids are in bed. The house is quiet. Think ahead to tomorrow, next week . . .

1. Can you anticipate areas where your child might make wrong choices?
2. What might you do to correct the situation when it happens?
3. Is there anything you can say or do BEFORE the situation arises to help your child be aware of considerations OUTSIDE himself or herself before making a choice?

When to let a child begin dating is a major crisis point for any parent, especially in our culture where dating opportunities occur earlier and earlier. Too early. In anticipation of the day when I would have to tell my daughter that she could NOT go out with a certain boy, I made up a game that we played for two years in advance. It went like this.

ME: "One day, Sweetie, some boy is going to come up to you and say, 'Hey, would you go to the dance with me?' And what are you going to say?"

SHE: *With a smile on her face.* "You have to ask my dad."

ME: "Then he will knock on my door and walk into my house and say, 'Sir, may I take your daughter to the dance?' And what will I say?"

SHE: "Get lost, buster!"

And we would both laugh and I would hug her and remind her that my job is to protect her until she is older.

We played that little game hundreds of times. Not ONE word ever changed.

Finally, after all that time, my sweetie came and asked me about going to a junior high dance with a boy. And I looked at her and said, "Well, I suppose you could have him come over and ask me."

She looked at me, and I looked at her, and she looked at me again and sighed. I hugged her, and she hugged me and said, "I know. You're just trying to protect me."

And I knew that I had anticipated well and had won my daughter in secret. No one else would ever know the battle that had been averted. (Unless of course I were to write about it in a book.)

3

Win your battles quickly.

CLEVERNESS has never been associated with long delays. If your child's obedience is long in coming, your energy will grow weak. When your wisdom is softened, your strength is exhausted and your energy spent, you will lose your ability to be the corrective force your child requires. Win your battles quickly while your resources and wits are the strongest. Too many parents fight the same battles for years. Don't wait for a small thing to turn into a big thing. Correct it while it is still small.

✍ Exercise #3

1. What improper behaviors occur over and over again?
2. What corrective measure needs to be implemented the next time you see this behavior, NO MATTER HOW SMALL it is?

One of my children was developing a habit of talking back to her mother and me. I realized that by sitting back and waiting I was creating a situation in which I might lose my daughter in an argument years from now. So Debbie and I agreed that the next time it happened, no matter how harmless it seemed at the time, we would treat it like a major offense and discipline her accordingly.

I went into my daughter's bedroom and told her about our concern and explained how we had decided to treat it in the future. She said she understood, but within hours she was doing it again.

The discipline, a serious spanking, was administered immediately and consistently (several times in fact that very day).

The remarkable thing was that in a matter of days my daughter was no longer talking back to us. At all.

By moving quickly we had stopped a habit that was sure to blow up in our faces sooner or later.

4

Impose your will upon your child.

D O not allow your child to force you to defend yourself. The purpose of discipline is to change behavior. Considering different opinions is well and good in most discussions, but not in discipline.

If there is something about your child's behavior that is causing him to flutter, narrow it down to precisely the problem, funnel it through the tips above to consider the right response, and address the problem with loving authority. It is important for your child to learn how to do what someone else wants.

Creating a nest for your child in which he or she never has to adjust to other people's desires dooms your child to future failure.

 **Exercise #4**

1. What area of your child's behavior is most confusing or uncomfortable to you?
2. Who could you talk to about it to get additional perspective?
3. What is the last thing you required your child to do "without asking questions?"

One of the most difficult things I've had to do as a parent is to create situations in which our children are required to do something WITHOUT ASKING QUESTIONS. I don't like having my children do things just because I say so. I like them to understand WHY I want something done. But to explain *every-* **163** *thing* does not prepare them for a life in which much is never explained. By making this a regular part of child-rearing, I can lovingly correct inappropriate reactions and help them develop the ability to follow instructions. But it remains one of the responsibilities that I don't enjoy.

5

Properly direct your anger.

TO discipline children properly, you MUST be angry. Your anger must burn within your soul and flare like fire from your nostrils, but it MUST be directed toward the proper things.

GET ANGRY at feeling hassled and how that twists your feelings of love for your children into frustration.

GET ANGRY at not having enough time to get to know and appreciate your children the way you know your best friend.

GET ANGRY because your marriage is screwed up and it's easier to take out your rage at the kids than your spouse.

GET ANGRY because you hate your job and have no energy left for the children when you walk in the door.

GET ANGRY because you become impatient when things aren't going the way you want them to go at home and you say things you later regret.

GET ANGRY at the RIGHT THINGS and do something about them so that you can save your kids' lives.

Often I sit up until two or three in the morning and "play." Our home has a quietness at that time of the morning that makes it seem unreal. I walk into the children's bedrooms and sit on their beds. Their little bodies, normally so full of

164

energy, appear helpless as they lie motionless across their sheets. I realize then their need for a protector, and I become angry at what I know is trying to get at them from the outside. Then I recall times when *I* have been the enemy, when I have spoken harsh words to them or displayed an insensitive spirit. I use those few quiet moments to reposition myself as their protector and to remind myself that the best way to protect my children from evil influences is to teach them what is good and to make it easy for them to choose what is good.

✍️ Exercise #5

1. Are you angry at your child?
2. Do you discipline in anger? Remember, discipline in anger is not discipline; it's an excuse for uncontrolled emotions.
3. How can you channel your anger in the right direction?
4. In what area is your child most vulnerable?
5. Of all the areas in which your child might require discipline, which is the most significant?

Don't be deceived. The battle you are fighting in your home is not to get a messy room straightened. It is not to get garbage cans taken out or dirty dishes washed or squabbling siblings to be at peace with one another. You are in a life-and-death battle. You have been given a human creature to launch. And there are a lot of things standing in the way of your success. Outside your door await enemies you don't even know. Keep them outside. Grow your child strong and healthy. Teach him how to protect himself and how to SOAR! Warn her of the deceptions of her adversaries and use discipline to hammer home the lessons she must carry with her the rest of her life. And remember to do it with wisdom, love, and sensitivity.

165

Drew's Story

We were excited when Drew started Cub Scouts, but we were mortified the first night after we picked him up. He sat sullen the whole way home. Then, in the middle of the night, he woke up screaming, "N-o-o-o-o-o-o-o."

We later found out what had happened.

Overwhelmed by the newness and size of the group of scouts, Drew had been unable to sit still. He didn't know what was expected of him, and it made him very uneasy. The leaders, hoping to teach him to sit still and concentrate, had put him in a time-out chair. This terrified Drew because he had no idea what he was supposed to do. Being punished in front of total strangers hurt him deeply. The leaders, instead of disciplining him, had deeply wounded him.

Getting STARTED

#17 Choose your own formula for discipline.
Will you . . .
☞ spank?
☞ suspend privileges?
☞ assign a task around the house?
☞ take something away?

#18 What things are happening around your
house that must be corrected. Are they
matters requiring discipline? If so . . .
☞ make a list
☞ have a family meeting
☞ describe the inappropriate behavior
☞ establish the consequences
☞ FOLLOW THROUGH!

Chapter Seven

Flying Straight

Helping Your Child Navigate Treacherous Skies

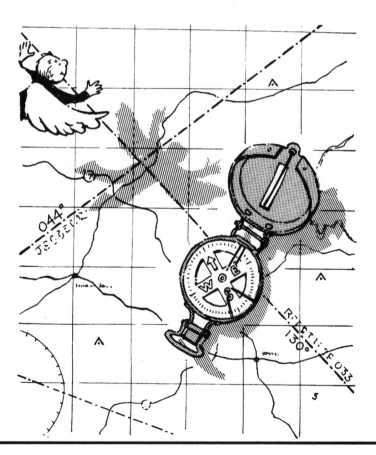

The formula for complete happiness is to be very busy with the unimportant.

—A. EDWARD NEWTON

IT'S A NORMAL MORNING IN YOUR HOUSE. Your little girl pulls herself sleepily out of bed. In the next thirty minutes she will have to decide what blouse to wear, what skirt or pants will match it, which socks to put on, what shoes to wear, what to eat for breakfast, what to wear in her hair, whether she will buy her lunch or take it, whether to carry her books or take her knapsack, whether her knee needs a bandaid, whether she has time to make her bed, and whether to put away her pajamas. These are only a few of the choices that greet her when she barely has her eyes open.

Then you enter the room and point out that her outfit doesn't match, her hair looks too ratty to go with that bow, her tennis shoes are filthy, there is NO way she can carry all those books without dropping them, and she had better put away her pajamas even if she has to miss the bus.

It's going to be a difficult day.

Navigational skills needed

You and your child face hundreds of choices every day. Some are simple ones, requiring little thought and having few consequences; others call for complex value judgments and have serious consequences if poor choices are made.

One mom described to me all the choices she had to make every day and how frustrated she was because for every choice she made, she had a child making a different choice. The confusion was eating her alive.

The average family faces more choices today than ever before, and most family conflicts have to do with these choices. Yet when was the last time you thought about the process you go through to make those decisions? Do you even *have* a process or do you just "make" them.

How well your child learns to fly will depend on how well he or she learns to navigate the treacherous skies of decision-making. With a little understanding of the decision-making process, you can help your child find his or her way through a maze of choices.

What's happening when our child chooses?

Not long ago I walked into our family room and discovered that my son had taken apart our hide-a-bed. *Entirely apart.* There were pieces everywhere. "Why did you do *that?*" I blurted.

"Because you said you were getting a new one."

"But we aren't getting a new one YET!"

"Oh."

Does it bother you when your child does something his or her own way? Maybe it even scares you. But I would be bothered if my child *didn't* want to do something his own way. Having preferences is as natural as having a certain eye color, a particular body shape, or a specific personality. But parents often fear that those preferences will result in bad choices. **GOOD choices bring the reality of life into balance with the preferences of life.** Here's how.

GOOD choices contain two ingredients: What I *want* to do AND what *ought* to be done.

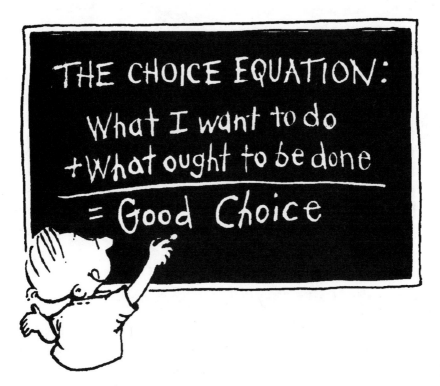

Those who pay attention to both parts of the equation have learned the first navigational skill needed to find their way through treacherous skies.

What *I WANT* to do

As little Wanda sits on the edge of her bed consider- ing what to wear to school, she may consider what the other children will wear, how certain colors look together, or what is considered "cool." But the more she thinks it over, the more she knows what she *wants* to wear. The resulting outfit may make you smile or roll your eyes. But there is no denying that she knows what she wants to do.

+ What *OUGHT* to be done

Sometimes the right decision will rest on considerations that have nothing to do with wants or preferences. A school dress code may make several of Wanda's choices meaningless. The weather may eliminate summer shorts from practical con- sideration. The *ought* factor is a significant piece of the choice equation in many ways.

= Good choice

Some parents' idea of a GOOD choice is one that agrees with theirs. A truly good choice, however, is one that balances **174**   *what the child **wants** to do and what **ought** to be done.* Remember, there is nothing wrong with allowing a child to exercise his or her preferences if the choice does not conflict with an important "ought."

What about you? Do you generally consider what OUGHT to be done as well as what you WANT to do before making a decision? Or are your decisions based mainly on what you want?

Making proper choices

Stacking your child's decisions is a true skill, one you'll use many times a day once you get the hang of it. Let's start with the one used most.

175

Automatic choices are decisions that have already been made by someone else.

Automatic choices are easy to identify. They are the non-negotiable ones. They appear to be choices but in reality the choice has already been made by another.

Which of the following decisions are automatic? (Put a check beside your choices here or in your workbook.)

- ☐ **Eating vegetables at mealtime**
- ☐ **Wearing a brown or black belt**
- ☐ **Calling home when late**
- ☐ **Cleaning room**
- ☐ **Not using drugs**
- ☐ **Sharing toys**
- ☐ **Saying "Yes sir" and "No sir"**
- ☐ **Washing the dinner dishes**
- ☐ **Not hitting siblings**
- ☐ **Doing homework alone**

Answers

✓ **Automatic.** *Eating vegetables* at mealtime is an
176 automatic choice if you have made it clear that the decision

has been made once and for all. It is non-negotiable if you have decided that it is. Children who think they can decide every evening at the dinner table whether or not to eat their vegetables need to learn that some choices have already been made for them.

Not-automatic. Whether to wear *a brown or black belt* is seldom an automatic decision. Unless there is a dress code, what color of belt to wear is not an automatic choice.

✓ **Automatic. In most families, *calling home*** if a child is going to be late is an established rule. Your child does not have to decide whether or not to find a phone and call you if he or she is running late. It is an automatic choice.

Not-automatic. *Cleaning his or her room.* This is a little tougher. While most parents wring their hands over the condition of their children's rooms, they have not made any automatic decisions to override the natural inclination some children have to live in messiness.

So unless you've made decisions to have your child pick things up off the floor every night before bedtime or dust the dresser every Saturday morning before playtime, this is not an automatic, unthinking, non-negotiable choice. If you have made these decisions, go ahead and check automatic.

✓ **Automatic. *Not using drugs.*** An easy one. Most parents agree with the medical community that drugs—whether alcohol, tobacco, or illegal substances—are harmful physically and emotionally. Your fear is that they will consider this a non-automatic choice, but for you, from the beginning this is an obvious automatic choice you'll teach your child.

Not-automatic. *Sharing toys.* What parent has not grimaced when his or her child has ripped a toy from another **177**

child's grasp and hissed, "Mine!" However, unless you have made a clear, once-and-for-all decision regarding this behavior, sharing is a choice your child must *want* to make.

Not-automatic. *Saying "Yes sir" and "No sir."* Most parents want polite children, but to make this automatic, you will have to decide how polite you want them to be. Responses like these don't happen naturally. They are carefully taught and reinforced over and over and over and over. Few parents choose to make this a priority. So unless you have, your child will have to choose whether this form of address is necessary.

✓ **Automatic. *Washing the dinner dishes.*** Clear-cut in your home? Does everyone understand the exact responsibilities—who does it on which nights and what it involves: clearing the table, drying the dishes, or putting them away? If so, score one for Automatic. If your dishwashing routine is more free-form, check Not-Automatic.

✓ **Automatic. *Not hitting siblings.*** Not ever. Under NO circumstances. Not allowed. Non-negotiable. Nothing to think about.

Not-automatic. *Doing homework alone.* If this has been decided as a non-negotiable, you may want to rethink it. Many children do not learn well by themselves and actually accomplish more when they are around other people.

Automatic choices can be wonderful navigational guides, but they have to be clearly communicated and never assumed, or you'll always be butting heads with that unique kid you have.

Here is a way to make sure that automatic choices are

made automatically:

AUTOMATIC CHOICES SHOULD BE . . .

1. **Clearly Communicated**

2. **Prominently Posted**

3. **Regularly Reaffirmed**

and . . .

4. **Made perfectly clear that . . .**

VIOLATORS WILL BE PROSECUTED
to the full extent of family law!

 **Exercise #1**

Do you have a list of automatic choices that apply to your child? Are they written down somewhere? If not, make a list of them now. Then make a date with your child to go over them.

Make regular visits to the list to reinforce the non-negotiable quality of the choices you expect your child to make automatically. Remember, children will do what they want to do unless they are clearly

179

instructed otherwise, and if you haven't been consistently clear they will be surprised if you become angry.

RIGHT choices are clear matters of right and wrong.

Right choices are attached to a higher authority. A parent may decide that vegetables are to be eaten nightly. That makes it an *automatic* choice but not necessarily a *right* choice. Eating vegetables is not a question of morality. When the child becomes an adult he or she may choose not to eat vegetables every night without breaking any moral law. Right choices, on the other hand, remain forever right.

Which of the following choices are a matter of right or wrong?

☐ 1. **Lying**

☐ 2. **Not answering when called**

☐ 3. **Not making the bed**

☐ 4. **Stealing**

☐ 5. **Cheating**

If you chose 1, 4, and 5, you are right. For our purposes here, there is never a situation when lying, stealing, or cheating is a proper choice.

Given an opportunity to lie, cheat, or steal, does your child think he or she has a choice? Of course. That is why the equation for making good choices is so important.

What I want to do
+ what ought to be done
= a good choice

Your child needs to understand that in AUTOMATIC choices and RIGHT choices, what he or she wants to do has zero value in the equation. Put another way, certain decisions—the ones you've made automatic or the ones that are right forever—do not take into consideration what *he or she* wants to do.

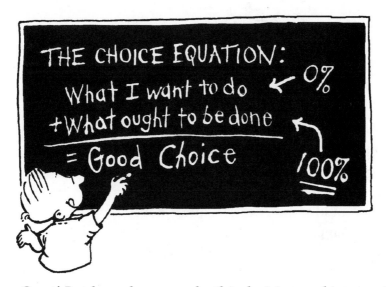

Great! But how do you make this decision-making magic happen? Communication and appropriate penalties are the answer.

When my son, Josh, was growing up, he would beat on his sisters when they bugged him. It made perfect sense to

181

him. If he popped them a good one, they left him alone. Until the next time. Finally, we sat him down and explained that hitting his sisters was not his choice to make; we had already decided for him that he was not to hit his sisters. We made it clear that if he chose to make his own decision in this matter that he would experience the "prearranged punishment." When it happened again, we carried out the punishment. And we did so consistently until Josh understood that he had no choice in the matter.

Communicating to your children *why* a certain choice is right or automatic and explaining the penalties to be carried out for making any other choice paves the way for good choices. These are important lessons to be learned for a lifetime of safe and sure navigating.

Right decisions are very serious matters, but don't expect your child to take them seriously if you don't. Do you frequently do what you WANT to do rather than what OUGHT to be done? Remember: Children listen, but they also watch.

SMART decisions balance what a person *wants* to do with what *ought* to be done.

In the course of a day we make many choices that are neither automatic nor a clear matter of right or wrong. But they are choices that require a SMART decision. And the number of smart choices to be made multiplies as we age.

No matter how old your children are today, they are older than they were yesterday. And each day that passes calls for more and more decisions to be made using their heads.

183

Take a look at the following situations that require a SMART choice. Are any of them familiar?

DAVID is fourteen. He wants to back the car into the driveway to surprise his dad. He has never backed a car up before. SMART choice?

LAUREN wants to use her new chalk set to draw a mural on the family room wall. SMART choice?

JIMMY wants to try carrying three plates of food to the table at the same time. SMART choice?

There is *no* magic formula to keep you or your child from making a poor choice. But now that you are learning how to truly see your child, you have the tools to understand the action. Remember that in *all* choices children make, their *first* inclination will be to use their natural abilities.

DAVID enjoys adventure, so that's what he is thinking about when he starts backing across the front lawn. He doesn't think about the shrubs and flowers lining the driveway or that it might be difficult to steer when his head is pointing to the rear.

LAUREN likes to create things, so the thought of drawing dinosaurs across the big, blank wall gets her all excited. She doesn't stop to think that maybe her mom won't be quite so excited about it.

JIMMY enjoys mastering a difficult task, so he sees only his grand entry into the dining room with the three plates, not a floorful of mashed potatoes.

SMART choices are often taught in a moment of failure.

Some decision-making skills are best taught after a crisis. You have your child's attention then. Take advantage of it. Talk. Then discuss other decisions that must be made in advance. Ask your child to consider two things before making such decisions:

1. What would he or she *like* to do in that situation?
2. What *ought* he or she do in that situation?

When the choice is not clearly a right decision or an automatic one, the SMART choice lies in balancing what your child would **like** to do and what your child **ought** to consider.

SMART choice things to remember

1

SMART choices are a learning playground.

SOONER or later your child will experience the consequences of his or her decisions. Use your home as a place to develop healthy, young adults by wisely teaching your children how to make SMART decisions.

185

One way is to allow them to fail and to learn from that failure. Another way is to begin moving some choices from the AUTOMATIC stack to the SMART stack. Talk about criteria for making decisions they weren't allowed to make for themselves previously. Be ready and willing to talk through poor decisions.

2

Hold your temper even if your child makes the same mistakes over and over again.

E XPECT that your child will repeatedly make wrong decisions. Due to certain strengths and abilities, he or she will always be set in a particular direction. If wrong decisions become dominant, make the SMART choice an AUTOMATIC decision and enforce penalties.

3

Relax. It's a bumpy ride.

A S your child gets older he or she will make some decisions that cause the hair on your neck to stand up. Refrain from sliding into the pilot's seat. Ride out the turbulence. You are involved in producing something more beautiful than a perfectly manicured lawn or a dust-free house. You are produc-

186 ing a well-disciplined child.

YOUR CHOICE decisions allow for the pure joy of unrestrained flight!

 "Do WHATEVER you want to do!"

How hard is it for you to say this to your child?

Are there decisions your child can make simply for his or her own delight, choices that are not automatic, not right or wrong, and not even necessarily smart? You better believe it.

Being a child can be a trying experience when parents think it is their job to make growing up a miserable ordeal. But that certainly was not what the Creator had in mind once upon a time. Think about his words to Adam:

"You are free to eat from *any* tree in the garden."

GENESIS 2:16

(Notice the AUTOMATIC choice in the second part of this well-known statement; it is complete with penalty for disobedience: "But you must not eat from the tree of the knowledge of good and evil, for when you eat of it you will surely die.")

It was within the Master Designer's plan to give ample opportunity for us to exercise choice—healthy choice—not necessarily a right or wrong choice—but a make-yourself-happy choice. "Go ahead and pick a tree—***any*** tree." We were intended to choose; so were our children.

For a child, there is something wonderful about making not the AUTOMATIC choice—although that is quite necessary—or the RIGHT choice—although that is a pleasing thing to do—or the SMART choice—which is always certainly the wise decision—but occasionally being allowed to just choose. A child loves to hear those wonderful words:

YOU CHOOSE!

✗ *What color would you like to paint your room?*

✗ *What shoes would you like to wear?*

✗ *What would you like for dinner tonight?*

✗ *Who would you like to sit next to?*

✗ *What would* you *like to watch on television?*

✗ *Would* you *like to climb into our bed and cuddle with us?*

A child who is NEVER allowed to choose is an accident waiting to happen. A parent who offers his or her children opportunities to make choices will experience moments that are some of the greatest joys of parenthood.

Stacks of choices, one on top of the other, that's the way our daily choices look. Our children will be making a hundred decisions a day by the time they leave our care.

On some days we wish we could make all of those decisions for them—to keep them safe and protect them from harm. But we can't. And on most days we wouldn't really want to if we could. The world is filled with adventure and requires our children to be involved and to react and to discover themselves through the very things that frighten us.

Learn to recognize the kinds of choices your child has to make. Teach your child which choices are not really choices at all. Help your child recognize the "rightness" of a particular decision. Raise your child to love a SMART choice.

And give your child one of the true joys of flight—making his or her own choice.

Lisa's Story

Sometimes it seems as if Lisa isn't choosing at all.

I asked her the other day if she wanted to play Nintendo or watch the "Aladdin" video. A simple question, I thought. What I forgot is how badly she wants to belong and to make others happy. When she answered, "I don't know. What do you want me to do?" I sighed and tried to think of a better way to rephrase the question. At a loss, I merely stated that I had no preference and would be happy as long as I knew I was doing what she wanted to do.

At this point she pleaded, "Dad, please, I really can't decide."

I guess we should be glad Lisa wants to please us so much, but sometimes we wish she would just express her true preferences.

#19 Begin your list of automatic and right choices today. What things do you expect to have happen around your house that you consider non-negotiable?

#20 What ten things could your child choose to do without any fear of making the wrong choice or being corrected?

Flying Higher to See the Bigger Picture

**Putting Your Child in the
Best Possible Position to Learn**

Everything is
a clue.

—ALEXANDRA STODDARD

MY CHILD IS A NATURAL LEARNER.

❑ **True**

❑ **False**

A natural learner? Is there such a thing? Kids who plow through piles of books and love every minute of it seem to make a good case for the possibility. Especially when placed alongside kids who doodle, pout, or daydream when given a book and told to sit at a desk.

Yet how do we know which of those two children is more gifted when it comes to learning? The daydreaming or fidgety child may have ten times the creativity or a hundred times the independence. Classroom experience rewards certain kinds of aptitude and completely misses other types which need just as much nurturing.

Does your child bubble over with the anticipation of learning history or math or being taught to diagram a sentence, solve an equation, or write a research paper? Why does the little boy who enjoys cutting a frog open in his own back yard get so fidgety when the class spends forty minutes memorizing the scientific names of the body parts?

There's a puzzle here.

Do educators and psychologists have the last word on how your child learns? If so, why do their words differ so much from one decade to the next?

While the question of learning may invite complex theories as to what takes place, when it takes place, and how to get **195** more of whatever it is whenever we want it, the one thing we can say absolutely about learning is this:

Most children are NOT natural learners.

Don't panic. This doesn't mean you have to throw that application to Yale into the trash.

Children who connect immediately with the knowledge being made available, no matter what the obstacles, are not the norm. In fact, natural learners like these are rare. Many children are stopped dead by such obstacles, and many of these obstacles are placed there by society and educators just when students are trying out their wings. The theories on which many of the country's educational systems base their classroom strategies are false.

Want proof?

Will you volunteer your child for a moment?

In the boxes below (or on the corresponding workbook page), check the answer that best describes your child:

HOW DOES YOUR CHILD . . .

STUDY FOR A TEST?
- ☐ Studies a little each evening to get ready.
- ☐ Practices writing out the answers over and over again.
- ☐ Stays after school and studies with the teacher.
- ☐ Pretends she has scarlet fever the day of the test.

DO HOMEWORK?
- ☐ Starts it as soon as he comes home from school.
- ☐ Closes the door to his room and studies intently.
- ☐ Begs you to take him to the library.
- ☐ Crams all of his books under the bed and plays Nintendo.

BEHAVE IN SCHOOL?
- ☐ Sits quietly at her desk all day and anticipates the next assignment.
- ☐ Is always first to raise her hand.
- ☐ Is the first one to school and the last one to leave.
- ☐ Spends all day passing notes to friends around the room.

What goes on in many schools has *nothing* to do with whether a child is smart or stupid. Too often it has to do with taking young beings designed to SOAR and shoving them behind tiny desks, putting imaginary tape over their mouths, and forcing them to stare at printed material and listen to hours of lectures when their fidgety, energetic little bodies need to be moving.

197

But before there were institutionalized learning environments called "schools" there was still learning.

Learning, *n., interaction with the world through life experiences.*

For all the knowledge and skills gained while studying the "3 R's," these basics (as in "back to the basics") are not the end-all of learning. The best teachers know this and infuse the classroom with real knowledge.

Do you remember that terrific teacher you had in the fourth grade? Mrs. Lovejoy made school so much fun that you got your best grades ever. She was a Master Teacher. Compare that experience to the year you had Ol' Lady Fudgebottom, who you thought hated your guts. I bet your grades weren't too good that year, were they? What made the difference? The curriculum certainly wasn't all that different.

When a teacher who doesn't understand how kids learn passes judgment on a ten-year-old child's aptitude by giving him a poor grade in geography, his parents are bewildered. They forget that the average classroom is an artificial experience which more often than not produces artificial results.

The *best* teachers, the Mrs. Lovejoys, were the ones who interrupted this artificial experience. They brought the classroom back to the real world. Grades were seldom an issue. Homework was a *means* not an *end*. Diagrams and charts were not the centerpieces of education. In their place were real life experiences. Numbers became musical notes. Body parts became dancing bones. The air in a history class became thick with the smell of musket powder as children imagined their ancestors dying for a cause they believed in. You were never quite the same after learning spilled into your life.

And you know what? It's time to say "thank you" to all the Mrs. Lovejoys.

Dear Mrs. Lovejoy,

Thank you for creating a healthy learning environment—not just a teaching environment—in your classroom. You taught me more than reading, 'riting, and 'rithmetic; you taught me to love learning! You made me curious about the world. You made me want to know more about everything. Instead of answering all my questions, you showed me where to find the answers. And in finding the answers, I found much more. The trail you started me down has led me further and further into knowledge.

I know I can never repay you for what you did for me, but I want you to know that all your efforts did not go unnoticed.

199

Unless your child is a natural learner or is lucky enough to have a Mrs. Lovejoy in every grade, he or she will collide with an educational system that does not understand learning. Oh, it believes in your child. And it wants your child to have an insatiable appetite for learning.

But the truth is that children want to learn only about things they are interested in. That's the nature of "wings." Children will fidget and daydream through anything they find uninteresting. And parents will hear about it. If not from their child then from the teacher.

We expect our children to be Superkids. All-around geniuses. And we sweat when the report cards show anything less. We not only want our children to *try* everything, we expect them to be *good* at everything—an impossible task for anyone—Albert Einstein, the president of the United States, Master Teachers, everyone. Yet we expect straight A's. Good at English? Great! But you must be good at math too!

So what's a parent to do?

Parents need their own STRATEGY

Parents must understand what NEEDS to happen in the classroom for learning to take place. And we must begin with the truth we know about our child.

Children who are not natural learners will most easily acquire information about things that interest them, things that help them develop and strengthen their own natural abilities.

Your role as a parent is to put your child into the best possible position to learn.

Don't spend your time wringing your hands about poor grades and unmet expectations. Don't worry about whether your child will handle life in the same way he or she handles the classroom. Even the best student must learn skills that have nothing to do with earning an A in math.

There are, however, some skills children MUST acquire regardless of their own natural enthusiasm. Some of these skills are obvious ones, such as reading and spelling and math. To navigate smoothly through life, every child must acquire them.

Do you hassle your child every night about homework and upcoming tests? Are your expectations reasonable for a child his or her age or are you expecting adult-level behavior?

Look for ways to position your child in the best possible place to learn, taking full advantage of his or her natural abilities. Every educational system, even the most frustrating ones, can be used to your advantage if you have a strategy.

Since there are so many things your child *must* learn for which he or she has no energy, parents need to use the educational system to their child's advantage. We do this by learning to teach SMART.

Getting ready to teach SMART

The real issue is not education in general; it's your child in particular. So you have to get involved. Not all at once, but **201** steadily. Teaching SMART may bother some educational professionals, but we're talking about YOUR child here, and your child is the reason the educational professionals are there. They should want to know all they can about your child. The Mrs. Lovejoys of the world will encourage your input; the Mrs. Fudgebottoms will not.

Here is the plan:

1

Make sure you understand YOUR CHILD.

THE fun part of what you are learning in *Born to Fly* is that it GROWS. As your understanding and observational skills develop, your ability to make sense out of what your child is doing becomes sharper.

How long should you wait before starting? Four weeks or longer are needed for all these ideas to seep in. Take the time to listen and observe and think about what we've been discussing.

2

Establish an ideal daily routine with your child.

WHAT situation at your house needs to be "fixed"? What would the situation be like if it were fixed? It's one thing to say something is not right. It's another to say how it should be. Keep your child's workbook nearby for a few days and scribble notes about the way you would like things to be around your house.

For example:

> ✗ *If your daughter is not finishing her homework before bedtime would it be better if you made her finish it before dinner?*

> ✗ *If your son is getting unusually poor grades in spelling would it help to have him spell the words for you every week BEFORE the test?*

Know what your ideal is. It may not be the ideal for your child, but you can adjust it as you begin to lay down guide-lines.

3

Identify the best places for your child to learn.

Recall some of the things you have learned about your child . . .

❖ Your child's strongest abilities.

❖ The places where your child works the best.

❖ The ways your child works the best with other people.

❖ The way your child uses time.

❖ The rewards your child needs.

IMAGINE that I just bumped into you on the street and asked you to describe your child in these five areas. Could you do it? If not, don't do anything else until you can. Pick one a day (if you aren't already doing this) and make observations about your child, as we discussed earlier. This information will guide you as you consider how to best position your child to learn.

The best position for learning is in a place where a child can use at least SOME of his or her natural ability. SO . . .

☞ A child who enjoys meeting needs would learn a lot while tutoring another student.

☞ A child who enjoys meeting requirements would learn a lot while completing workbooks.

☞ A child who enjoys overcoming challenges would learn a lot if given something difficult to do.

☞ A child who enjoys interacting with others would learn a lot by talking with other kids.

Your observations and strategies put you in a position to actually DO something. So here we go.

Encourage your child's BEST response

Your nest is made out of things that give it warmth and stability yet allow it to remain flexible. By pushing and mushing it into different shapes you can create an environment that encourages your child's best response.

 ## Change family schedules.

If your child seems to have more energy *before* dinner, eat later in the evening so he can finish his homework before you sit down to eat. If your child seems to have more energy right

205

before bedtime, schedule bedtime for a little earlier and allow her to read and study while sitting up in bed. I know parents who have done both with great success.

Rearrange furniture.

Furniture placement has a surprising effect on children and adults alike. One teacher I know sets up the reading area of her classroom on a warm-colored carpet with a big bean bag chair and a low-hanging lamp. It makes a kid want to run right over, snuggle down, and read like crazy. The teacher uses it as a reward for children who finish their work.

Pretty smart, huh?

Almost. But why not let the excitement of the place stimulate learning rather than require the child to learn something to get there? Why not allow children to work on their assignments in the chair. Wouldn't *that* be exciting? Who says children shouldn't have fun *while* learning?

Look for opportunities at home to rearrange your furniture to create learning spaces. Where does your child study best? What kind of space does he need for reading? Where is she best able to concentrate on math? Scoot the furniture around and turn the best places into "spaces" to learn.

Synchronize your needs with those of your child.

A whole lot of learning can take place in unusual situations. Put your child in the front seat of the car and watch how interested she becomes in *everything* whizzing by. You can use that energy for learning. Take her along to the store and have her bring her spelling list. She may show a lot more interest in reviewing those spelling words in the car than sitting at the kitchen table being cross-examined as if she were on a witness stand. Synchronize your schedule with her needs and watch how much valuable time you pick up.

Where do YOU learn the best? What is YOUR best place to think? Did you ever wonder why you did so well once you got OUT of school?

Use new eyes and fresh thoughts.

And if you want to recognize someone who teaches smart, you will have to teach smart yourself.

EIGHT principles of teaching SMART

1

Stop. Look. LISTEN!

D ON'T talk to your child if he is doing something else. Get his attention first. To give directions or talk to children **207** who obviously are not listening is to invite frustration. Assess the situation you're in. Is it a good learning place? Is everybody calm and ready? Is someone yelling from another room? What do you need to hear from your child? Both sides need to talk, not just you. What might your child need to tell you?

2

Look your child in the eye.

GAINING your child's eye contact is a challenge. What do you need to do to get it and maintain it? Get down on the floor? Wave your arms? Touch her arm? Learning is enhanced when eye contact is maintained. You'll have more teaching success if you concentrate on your child's eyes rather than on her fidgeting little body.

3

Flip off the autopilot.

EVERY opportunity to learn is a brand new experience for your child. It may be boring for you, but it's your duty to make the subject interesting. Master Teachers instinctively know how to freshen up boring subjects. They have to repeat their subjects at least yearly, so they learn to be inventive. Change the scenery, serve hot chocolate while the workbook is being completed, play some music. Since few children learn naturally, they need our help to stay focused.

208

4

Get a reaction!

ENCOURAGE your child to shout his spelling words. Let him stand up and raise his hands over his head while he answers questions. Physical action helps a child focus on the material at hand. If you are giving instructions or explaining how to do a problem, ask for a reaction. "Tell me what I just told you" or " Now YOU do this problem for me."

5

Create a presence.

USE your size, eyes, voice, and hands as teaching tools. You are bigger than your child. Use your size to your advantage. Your voice can go higher or lower, express anger or joy, excitement or boredom. Your hands can touch, hold out items to show, draw something, or clap. They create a link between you and your child. In creating a presence, you take control of the space you are sharing with your child.

**PRESENCE enables you
to *reward* children,
communicate with them,
gain a reaction
from them.**

209

A Master Teacher who controls his or her teaching space by creating a presence does not have to compete with distractions.

Build a bridge.

CHILDREN are on the opposite side of a deep chasm filled with countless learning experiences. Don't expect them to jump in with both feet and start swimming across. Instead build a bridge and start leading them across. A few minutes spent chatting, gaining perspective, or doing something physical goes a long way toward good bridge-building.

BELIEVE these principles.

THESE principles are navigational guides to teaching SMART. You have to believe them and understand them. If you don't, and if your child is not one of the lucky few who are natural learners, you will not be in a position to help your child through this critical loop. You play an important role in your child's learning opportunities; if you don't believe this, you will be just like the parents who, after reading the following in *Better Homes & Gardens,* decided to stay away from their child's classroom experience.

Better Homes & Gardens
September 1991
**PARENTING RESOLUTIONS
FOR THE NEW SCHOOL YEAR**

- I'll stay away from my child's homework.
- If my child forgets something, I'm not going after the bus.
- I WON'T do major projects with my child, even if it means a slightly lower grade.
- I'll teach my child the Three R's of respect, responsibility and resourcefulness and let the teacher teach the Three R's of reading, 'riting and 'rithmetic.

8

Relax!

MOST of all, relax. Just relax. There is really no pressure. Most of what you feel comes from trying to meet the standards of an educational system that may be a bit out of sync with your child and your family. But your child is going to be just fine. Believe it or not, when your child is thirty-five no one will really care what grade he or she received in spelling at age nine. The educational community is going through a metamorphosis right before our eyes, because of such facts of life. Don't get caught up in it. Relax and enjoy your child as you get better at teaching SMART.

Specific ways to position children to learn

 Train them to interact with adults.

How do you want your children to interact with adults? Their natural way may not correspond with what you think is appropriate. DECIDE what you consider to be healthy and appropriate interaction so you can help your child acquire those skills.

Do you want your child to shake hands firmly, say "yes sir" and "no sir," be quiet unless spoken to, answer the phone a certain way, not talk back to adults (please, make sure your child knows what "talking back" is!), only speak about adults in a certain manner? What do you consider healthy? These decisions and patient instruction by you position your child to learn from all the adults around him or her.

Teach them to separate from you.

Don't drop your child off at school or preschool for a long period of time without any preparation for the experience. For some children, their natural abilities make it difficult for them to be suddenly separated from mom and dad. Know your child and make opportunities for short periods of separa-

212 tion before the child is expected to spend a whole day away.

MEMO
On Homework

Homework may be the most misused teaching method in education today. Studies long have concluded that little if any SIGNIFICANT LEARNING takes place during the exercise of homework, yet many teachers build hours upon hours of homework into their lesson plans. Model schools are now popping up around the country where NO HOMEWORK is allowed in the entire school. Teachers are left with only the opportunity to teach the student *in the classroom.* The results are more than encouraging.

What's wrong with homework?

1. No immediate feedback to the student. By the time the student gets back the results, the learning window has already closed.

2. Doesn't relate to actual class content. Homework is often given as a form of busy work with little connection with actual class content.

3. Rules of homework are ABSURD—created out of culture and duty. Some teachers require one hour a day, some require forty minutes per class, some assign it every other night, and some never assign homework on weekends.

4. There is NO TEACHER present. The whole purpose of a teacher is to initiate learning. No teacher—no learning!

Think about all the arguments you have had with your child about homework. Was your concern more about learning or about obligation to our educational system?

Teach them to attend to a task.

Most children do not have the natural abilities to begin, follow through, and finish a task. You want to prepare them for the expectations that await them in the classroom by helping them understand the three phases of a task:

- ❖ **STARTING**
- ❖ **DOING**
- ❖ **FINISHING**

Help your child identify these different phases as he or she does normal activities around the house. For instance, "Now you are starting to vacuum the floor." A little later, "Now you are doing the floor." And as they are winding up the cord, "Now you are finishing the floor!" Since most people don't do all three naturally, there is usually little sense when a task is left incomplete, especially for a child. Many of you reading this book have been watching your teenager half-clean up her room for four years now. It's time to teach her the three phases of attending to a task.

 ## Train them to delay personal gratification.

Children want what they want and they want it NOW! (Hmm. Did I say children? Okay, even as adults we never quite correct this problem.) It is nevertheless important to teach our children the virtue of patience. By deliberately attending to some other matter for a while before satisfying a child's driving desire, parents can quell the child's need for immediate gratification (and maybe even learn some patience of their own in the process). During the course of an average day there

will be dozens of situations when your child will want something and want it NOW. Choose a few appropriate ones and redirect the energy of your child's desire. Doing so will help your child learn to delay personal gratification.

 ## Balance your home's emotional state.

You control the emotional thermostat in your nest. You will probably be making some family or personal decisions in the quiet of the evening tonight. What is the atmosphere in your home like? Is there a lot of yelling? Are things disorganized? Is everyone always late getting out the door in the morning? Is getting your children off to school a good time or is it World War III every day?

Refuse to let the atmosphere of your home damage the emotional health of the people living in it.

An eight-year-old who is yelled at from the time he gets up until the moment he slams the front door on his way out to the bus is in no shape to spend an entire day in a classroom. Period.

 ## Teach them to take directions.

Take out the garbage!
Clean your room!

Are those directions or commands? You are the instructor in one of your child's most important courses: *How to take directions.* Treat it seriously. Taking directions is one of the most important courses your child is enrolled in at home.

NEVER assume that a command can be translated into directions. Make your instructions as complete as possible. "Clean your room" is a command. So turn it into directions: "This morning I want you to make your bed, vacuum the floor, and dust your dresser. They need to be done by 10:30. I'll be in to check at that time." Remember to use a certain teaching SMART tip from this chapter: Gain eye contact and a reaction.

 ## Be your child's champion.

Be active in your child's classroom and school. Know how your child's teacher teaches. Sit in the class. Watch and listen. Know what you should and should not tolerate. A mom asked me the other day what she should do about her nine-year-old whose new teacher was, by the mom's own observation, having a bit of trouble. The teacher yelled at the kids, had little or no group activities in class, and assigned lots of homework. After the first four days of the school year, her daughter didn't want to go to school. Should the mother say anything? *What would you do?*

My response to the mother was: "Sit in on your child's class and confirm your suspicions. If they hold true, get your daughter out of that class and into the one across the hall." You have to be a champion for your child. Know what you can change and what you can't stand. Luckily, this woman had an easy option. After a thirty-minute meeting with the principal the switch was negotiated. Don't be afraid to speak up. This is your child caught in the middle. Know what you can tolerate and what you can't. I know some parents who make the rounds the first week of school to tell the teachers they are not going to allow homework to control their children's lives. As you might imagine, such parental intervention makes for interesting discussion. Don't be afraid to champion the cause. But don't be unnecessarily antagonistic.

ONE LAST THOUGHT...

What happens in the classroom turns a lot of potentially happy homes into a disaster. After children turn six years of age, they spend more time in a classroom with a teacher and twenty-five or more kids than they spend in their own home. It's not easy, even for the small number of children who are natural learners. Help them get ready and be ready yourself to teach SMART!

217

Drew's Story

We were pleased when Drew brought home an "A" on his report card in science. Just the semester before we had badgered him for weeks about bringing up his grade in that class and he came home with only a "C" to show for it. Obviously all of our prodding had not paid off. We asked Drew to explain to us his sudden success, but all he could do was shrug his shoulders.

Several days later his father and I were sitting with Drew's teacher at a parent conference. She apologized for the temporary overcrowding in the classroom and explained that they were making do by taking six of the children, including Drew, down to the gym and having science class around a little table.

"O-h-h," I said. "That explains it."

Drew loved to interact with other people, and now he had a chance to learn science in a place where he could talk and ask questions whenever he wanted to. Suddenly he was learning science in spite of himself.

As we were driving home we wondered aloud whether such a simple shift could help Drew in some other classes he was having difficulty in.

#21 Make a list of the subjects your child is taking in school. Looking at each one, evaluate your child's ability to do what is required for each class. What help will he need? Where will she have trouble? What strategy can you put into place to help your child complete each class successfully? REMEMBER: Your child doesn't need straight A's to prove that he or she is learning or excelling.

#22 Start preparing for your next parent-teacher conference. What does the teacher need to know about your child? What things can you suggest that would help your child learn? How can you make these suggestions without making the teacher defensive?

Worm Hunting and Other Skills

Teaching Your Child to Be Smart, Safe, and Sane in a World Filled with Predators

Grant me
to become
beautiful in the
inner man.

—SOCRATES

**I**T'S NOT SAFE OUT THERE.

And before long we'll have to send our little ones out there alone to fend for themselves. First kindergarten, then junior high, high school, college, and marriage. Each move takes them further from the safety of our protective wing. I wonder, was it easier for our parents to send us off than for us to tell our children good-bye or is it always easier for the generation leaving than for the one being left?

Survival of the fittest

The point is moot, I suppose, because all too soon our children will be grown up and going out on their own. Our sons will have to choose food that will keep them alive. Our daughters will have to choose television programs that won't permanently warp their moral conscience. They will have to choose what time to go to bed and how much sleep they need. And they'll have to remember to call home every evening. (We wish!) In other words, there is coming a time when *we won't be able to "help" them anymore*. What do I mean? Simply this:

The most important investments you make in your child's life will be made during the first eighteen years.

I don't mean, of course, that you won't be able to influence your child or have an important place in his or her life. But your chance to love and nurture that unique being toward becoming a successful, healthy soaring adult comes only in the early years.

The following "Soaring Proverbs" will help you instill life-saving principles into that young life as early and as often as possible. If during those early years you find moments to teach your precious child these lessons, the chances are better, much better, that he or she will stay smart and safe and sane.

Make Good Friends

Do not make friends with a hot-tempered man, do not associate with one easily angered, or you may learn his ways and get yourself ensnared.

PROVERBS 22:24–25

FOR a while it's easy, isn't it? You choose all the friends your child plays with. Then one day he or she brings home a kid you've never met, and nothing is ever quite the same. It's frightening when children begin to choose their own friends, but that's the way it has to be. Yet the ability to choose good friends will affect their entire lives. Since we can't go on choosing our children's friends, it's essential that we teach them the importance of having the ***right friends.***

Flight Lessons

Talk to your child about the following questions:

★ *What IS a friend?*

★ *How do you choose a friend?*

★ *Can you be friendly without being a friend?*

★ *What things should people look for in a friend?*

★ *What should we do with friends who are not "good" friends?*

Use Your Own Stuff

*The borrower is
servant to the lender.*
PROVERBS 22:27

WHAT'S mine is mine and what's yours is mine." Your child may find it hard to distinguish between "my stuff" and "your stuff" when the prevailing mindset is "I WANT your stuff!"

The line between owning and borrowing has become blurred even for adults in these days of easy credit and unlimited borrowing power. Children need to develop principles of ownership and be allowed to manage their own property. They need to be taught that in most cases it is better to go without something than to borrow to get it.

Flight Lessons

★ *What responsibilities come with owning something?*

★ *Does your child own his or her toys?*

★ *Is your child free to withhold them if he or she chooses?*

★ *How can you teach your child the reality of "waiting" instead of "borrowing?"*

★ *What should your child do if someone asks to borrow something of his or hers?*

Don't Fly Solo

*As iron sharpens iron,
so one man sharpens another.*
PROVERBS 27:17

THE last thing children want to hear at the moment their wings are unfurling and they are beginning to soar is a second opinion. They see no reason to ask how to do it or whether or not it should be done. But as you and I have learned through personal experience, most bad decisions could have been prevented by getting a second opinion.

Even though budding adults seldom care what anyone else thinks, your job includes teaching a healthy consideration for other opinions. And remember, flying alongside your child means giving support as much as it does warning of oncoming traffic.

Flight Lessons

★ *When is your child most likely to listen to somebody?*

★ *Who is your child most likely to listen to?*

★ *How does your child react when you give advice?*

★ *When does your child hide what he or she has done?*

227

Tell the Truth

*An honest answer is
like a kiss on the lips.*
PROVERBS 24:26

PERHAPS nothing you can do will affect your child's life as deeply as planting and nurturing an automatic leaning toward honesty. Honesty doesn't come naturally. Check the Ten Commandments if you think it does. Choosing the truth first is a lesson that must be learned early. If you wait until your children find out that they can have many of the things they want if they bend the truth a bit, the task will be much more difficult. The ability to recognize our own tendency to lie and to turn instead to the truth brings with it a lifetime of blessing.

Flight Lessons

★ *In what situations does your child have the hardest time telling the truth?*

★ *Do you make it a habit to find out the truth or do you let your children get away with lying?*

★ *Is your discipline for lying one of the most severe disciplines you administer?*

★ *Does your child understand clearly that a lie will never be tolerated?*

★ *Does your child also understand that a measure of grace is always waiting when he or she chooses to tell the truth?*

Control Yourself

*Like a city whose walls are broken down
is a man who lacks self-control.*
PROVERBS 25:28

PEGGY Noonan, in the September 1990 issue of *Forbes* magazine, wrote, "Our ancestors believed in two worlds, and understood this to be the solitary, poor, nasty, brutish and short one. We are the first generations of man that actually expects to find happiness here on earth, and our search for it has caused such unhappiness."

What does making our children happy mean? Does it mean giving them everything they want? Are you trying to make every Christmas bigger than the one before? It's okay, you know, for children NOT to have dessert EVERY night. While it seems almost unAmerican, teaching our children lessons in self-denial and self-control are some of the best, most long-lasting gifts we can give them.

Flight Lessons

★ *Is your child developing self-control?*

★ *Can your child withhold desire for something without throwing a tantrum?*

★ *Are you daily helping your child to exercise muscles of self-control which hold those wings of self-indulgence in check?*

Don't Do Anything When You're Mad

*A hot-tempered one
commits many sins.*
PROVERBS 29:22

ONE of the maddening things about raising a little one is that when the temptation to be angry is the strongest is when we need to have the clearest head.

Inevitably, your child will lose his or her temper. Some children more often than others. It is in the heat of that moment that your focus should be the sharpest, because that is the moment to teach. *An angry child will make bad decisions and will continue to do so as an adult.* Your child needs lessons on anger-control to use both before getting angry and while angry. And that's hard because that's usually when you want to yell back. But don't. Teach instead.

Flight Lessons

★ *When does your child get angry?*

★ *Does everybody start shouting?*

★ *What is the best thing to do when your child gets angry? Have your child sit for a minute or two and calm down?*

★ *Why is it important that your child NEVER leaves your home angry?*

Think before You Speak

Do you see a man who speaks in haste?
There is more hope for a fool than for him.

PROVERBS 29:20

W HY does it take us so long to realize the value of thinking before we speak? If we could collect all the messes we could have avoided by thinking first, imagine how high the pile would be.

Does your child think before speaking? Try developing exercises that emphasize thinking rather than speaking.

Flight Lessons

★ *When does your child's speech get him or her into trouble?*

★ *Does your child jump into conversations without regard for what other people are saying?*

★ *Have you ever discussed with your child how to listen to other people?*

★ *What games would help you teach your child how to ask questions and gather information from people? For example: Tell your child you want to know his or her opinion about something in five minutes and have your child use the time to think about his or her response.*

231

Get Up and Finish Your Work

A little sleep, a little slumber, a little folding of the hands to rest—and poverty will come on you like a bandit and scarcity like an armed man.
PROVERBS 24:33–34

CHILDREN have all the enthusiasm in the world for activities that allow their natural wings to spread and lift them into full flight. They have NO ENERGY at all for anything else. The world outside is not like your nest, all carefully assembled to provide just the right opportunities and motivations and encouragement for your child. The skies outside are unfriendly, and expectations are high and task-oriented. Our children will not always have someone cheering them on. They will find very few opportunities for begging off or sleeping in. Too many adults learn this late, to their detriment.

Flight Lessons

★ *Do you require your child to do things around the house that your child doesn't want to do?*

★ *Does your child take video breaks before finishing a chore and never get back to the chore?*

★ *Do you make your expectations clear?*

★ *How can you teach your child that part of growing up is taking on more and more responsibility for things which he or she may not have much enthusiasm for?*

Treat Mom and Dad with Respect

The eye that mocks a father, that scorns obedience to a mother, will be pecked out by the ravens of the valley.
PROVERBS 30:17

YOUR child is too busy spreading those wings to be concerned about respect. That means *you* have to take it seriously. The reason for teaching your children to respect you is not for your own ego; it's for their protection. When your children yell at you, call you stupid, don't pay attention to your directions, or even hit you, trust me, it's not cute. And it's not "just a phase they're going through." It's a sign that something is seriously wrong.

In making such responses unacceptable you must replace them with acceptable ones. To do this you must model respectful behavior. Let your children know that you too are under authority—to your boss, pastor, elders of your church, or government officials. Then demonstrate respectful behavior toward these individuals. It is not enough to demand respect. You might as well demand that your children enjoy cleaning their rooms. Children learn respect by how *you* show respect.

Flight Lessons

★ *What things would your child do differently if he or she respected you?*

★ *What things does your child do that are respectful and what things are not?*

★ *How are you going to change the expectations suddenly rather than gradually?*

233

Take Care of the Kid without a Coat

He who gives to the poor will lack nothing, but he who closes his eyes to them receives many curses.
PROVERBS 28:27

ONE of the problems of living in America today is the mindset that says people who are less fortunate than we are have either failed to take advantage of the marvelous opportunities afforded everyone or that they cannot be trusted.

Neither is true. Children need to develop an awareness of people less fortunate than themselves and an understanding of their responsibility toward them. Our family has started holding "Angel Hunts." We drive around and look for someone who needs something—like food or gloves or shoes—and we try to meet that need. To an adult, all the needs may seem overwhelming, but children can see the good a small thing like gloves can do and can experience the true joy of helping someone in need. If they sacrifice something of their own, it makes the experience even more valuable.

Flight Lessons

★ *How can you develop a sensitivity in your child for those less privileged? Get involved in a hospital or nursing home? Have your own "angel hunt?" Give away presents to a needy family at Christmas? "Adopt" a child at a local orphanage? Things like this don't just happen; they require careful planning.*

Love My Words

When I was a boy in my father's house, still tender, and an only child of my mother, he taught me and said, "Lay hold of my words with all your heart; keep my commands and you will live."

PROVERBS 4:3–4

SOMEWHERE in all of the hustle and bustle and rustling around, you have to CONNECT with your child. Ultimately, being a parent is not about broken toys, fighting brothers and sisters, and messy rooms. There is something ENORMOUS going on in your home. You and your child have a relationship that makes the angels in heaven jealous. Your child needs to see you as the person who is passing on to him or her the meaning of life itself. And you need to see your child as a tender shoot, sprouting firm and strong as he or she receives nourishment from your words and wisdom. I know, it takes some imagination to see things that way when your kid is standing in the middle of a dirty clothes pile, but try. Really try.

Flight Lessons

★ *When was the last time you spent some quiet time with your child?*

★ *How often do you share with your child your concerns about life as well as the things you've learned?*

★ *Does your child know the passions of your heart?*

★ *What changes do you need to make in your OWN life so you'll have something worthwhile to pass on to your child?*

CONSIDER THIS

YOU have only 6,570 days between the day your child is born and the day he or she turns eighteen. If your child is nine, you have only 3,285 days left. Make them all count. It won't be long before you'll be willing to pay a million dollars to have just one of these days back again.

Thank God every day for the opportunity you have to kiss your little one on the cheek, to move a tricycle, to watch your daughter model your clothes, to make a peanut butter and jelly sandwich, to take your son's temperature, to change a diaper, to cuddle on the couch, to have your child fall asleep in your lap, to stop sisters from arguing, to yell at the kids to pick up their clothes, to wipe away their tears, to spank your son, to play hopscotch . . .

It just doesn't get any better than this!

I'll look for your child in the skies.